Of all Hawaii, I like photographing Kauai best. Possibly because it is Kauai where I began photographing Hawaii and learned what an island is and the special magic of being on an island. It was in 1946, when I sailed with friends for Kauai aboard the inter-island steamer *Wai'ale'ale* on the overnight voyage from Honolulu. I remember paying for a cabin, but never stepping inside, for I stayed awake all night on deck waiting for my first view of Kauai at dawn. With food, sleeping bags and tents on pack frames we made ourselves, we hiked across the island from Puhi to Hanalei on the Power Line trail and on into remote Kalalau Valley. For a week, my friends and I were the only people sharing the spectacular wilderness of Napali and Kalalau.

Kauai has changed considerably in the years since postwar plantation days—yet in significant ways, Kauai has not changed in any way. The natural beauty of Napali and Kalalau I first saw twenty five years ago is as yesterday. Awa'awapuhi Valley has still to shelter a camper. Mt. Wai'ale'ale, bold and powerful at dawn, still hides itself inside wet tradewind clouds every afternoon, while rain from the wettest place overflows Alakai Swamp into Waimea Canyon. It has always been so.

On a summer dawn, the summit of Wai'ale'ale is often clear. At all other times the mountaintop bog is the rainiest place on earth.

It is said that the first Hawaiians discovered Kauai perhaps 1200 years ago. The British Captain Cook stopped by Kauai over 200 years ago, on his way north from Tahiti. His journals soon told the world about this paradise of the Pacific. Over 100 years ago, American planters began growing the first commercial sugar cane at Koloa. Their successors overthrew the corrupt Hawaiian Kingdom leading to democratic government in Hawaii. In the years since statehood, trans-pacific jetliners have carried millions of happy tourists to Kauai. In turn, everyone has stepped somewhat harshly on the land—Hawaiians, sugar planters, ranchers and tourists, yet the Kauai landscape still seems like it always was.

The perpetual bog of Alaka'i swamp, in the rain shadow of Wai'ale'ale, allows the 'ohi'a lehua tree to survive only as a dwarf of its magnificence elsewhere.

Because there is no road winding completely around the island, there is still a mystery beyond the end of the road—the island we search for, but never quite find because it is beyond our reach. It is best that no road circles the island; that there are places we cannot walk; places where even a helicopter or raft cannot land, because then that special kind of place we yearn for, but never see, would be revealed. That wonderous world beyond the end of the road would no longer be a fascinating and mysterious land. It is not necessary, that we must see and touch all the islands' wildness—it is only necessary to know that wildness still exists.

No one walks across the island today. Many hike the Napali trail, but as many more ride Papillion helicopters and Zodiac rafts into Kalalau. When visitors deplane from inter-island jets, after the 25 minute flight from Honolulu, they climb into tour buses or rental cars. A few try hitchhiking with a pleading expression. Everyone is asking the way to the end of the road.

The fast way to the end of the road is not the way to know Kauai—it is the way to miss what an island is. For the end of the road at Polihale, Koke'e or Ke'e is not Kauai. The island is the people and places in between. The road on the way is Kauai. No need to travel to the end.

Beyond the end of the road at Ke'e are the sea cliffs of Napali, the island's face to the north.

The water that carries leaves in Wainiha stream, or sinks quickly into the sand at Polihale, assumes the texture of its environment.

It may be romanticism to find ideal beauty only in nature. In some ways it is satisfying to not know everything about nature; to not have seen it all—to be constantly searching for the ideal. Otherwise the serenity induced by nature may quickly dissipate should we return from a successful search.

In some ways it seems better to not see everything about an island that we know to be geographically finite; like the remote wilderness of Alakai swamp and beyond Nu'alolo and Miloli'i where we cannot see around the corner. The Napali that remains unseen from the lookout at Koke'e and in our imagination must be ever more beautiful than any photographer shows it to be. I like the Kauai that surrounds itself with clouds every afternoon and disappears after dark, when the menehune awake to prepare island landscapes for next days viewing, always saving the best to hide from us in places we cannot touch or be.

It is said the legendary menehune people of another, older time constructed Alakoko fishpond in one night's work.

The waves that sweep upon the sand, spreading shoreward like ancient ali'i capes; exotic pink poha vines smothering ancient acacia koa; even thorny blackberry spreading across the indiginous forest of Kokee like an alien invasion from another planet; all mix together before the camera into an exciting panorama of photographic images complimenting perfectly the mix of island people and ethnic experiences.

On a rising tide, the final surf sweeps quickly ashore at Barking Sands, resting momentarily atop the coral sand before disappearing within.

The great mountain swamp of Alakai. The innermost reaches of Awaʻawapuhi valley where cattle have never grazed. Crumbling ruins of Russian forts and ancient Hawaiian temples. Sugar and papaya. The bright, green fields of Princeville pastures and flickering torches in Grace Guslander's coconut grove. Taro in Hanalei valley. The *Bali Hai* cliffs of Haʻena, high mountain waterfalls and cold trout streams. Romantic hidden beaches, surfing waves and coral reefs. Gentle people on an island surrounding the wettest place on earth. Polihale, Anahola, Waiʻaleʻale, Nawiliwili…

If we could not see Kauai for ourselves, we would never believe it.

Volcanic land, colored green by uluhe fern, rises above Hanalei beach like a stairway.

KAUAI
Hawaii's Garden Island

Text and Photography by
ROBERT WENKAM

A Wenkam / Candēre Book

Rand McNally & Company   Chicago · New York · San Francisco

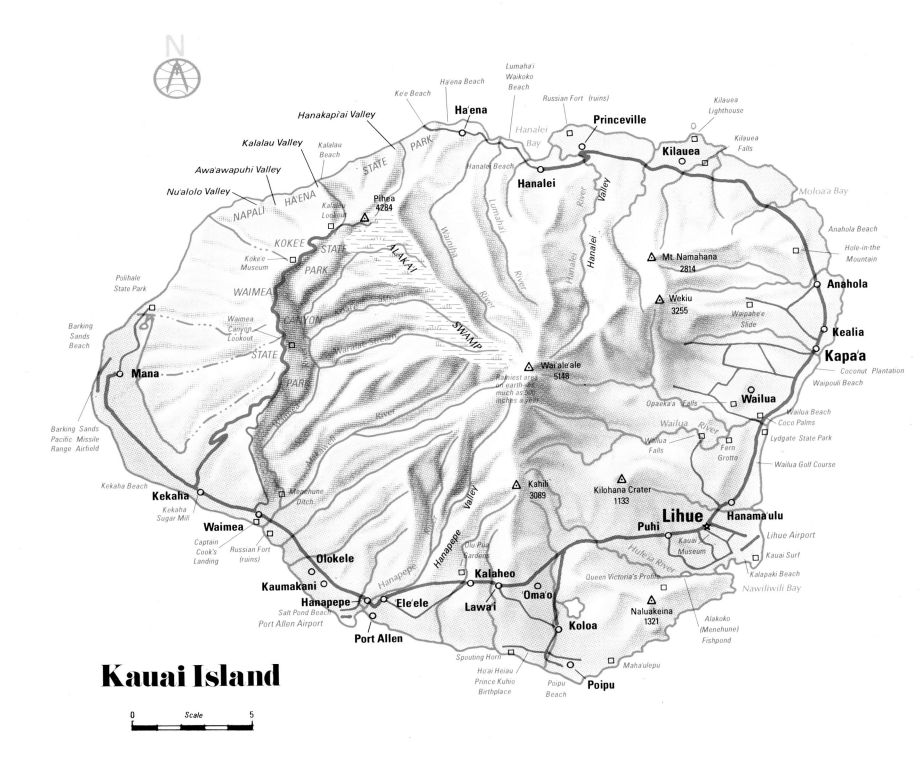

Kauai Island

0 — Scale — 5

Quote from *God's Own Junkyard*, by Peter Blake,
© copyright 1964, by permission
Holt, Rinehart and Winston, New York.

Quote from *Hawaii*, by James A. Michener,
© copyright 1959, by permission
Random House, Inc., New York

Quotes from *The Kumulipo*, translated
by Martha Beckwith, by permission
Bishop Museum, Honolulu, Hawaii.

Editor ● Herb Luthin, Chicago
Design ● Robert Wenkam, Honolulu
Composition ● The Production Centre, Honolulu
Photographs ● Hasselblad, Ektachrome 64

Other books by Robert Wenkam

Honolulu Is An Island
    Photographs and text by R. Wenkam

Hawaii The Big Island
    Photographs and text by R. Wenkam

New England
    Photographs and text by R. Wenkam

Hawaii
    Photographs and text by R. Wenkam

Micronesia: Island Wilderness
    Photographs by R. Wenkam. Text by K. Brower

Maui: The Last Hawaiian Place
    Photographs and text by R. Wenkam

Micronesia: Breadfruit Revolution
    Photographs by R. Wenkam. Text by B. Baker

Kauai and the Park Country of Hawaii
    Photographs and text by R. Wenkam

Contents

Acknowledgments

In researching the ecological history of Kauai, trying to find out why the island looks the way it does, I found much written about what people did *on* the land but little about what happened *to* the land. Political histories and historical novels about Hawaii are abundant, but none told me why the island we see today is so very unlike the islands first settled by early Polynesian explorers.

I went to government file cabinets, read family correspondence, and waded through water-soaked monthly reports reserved by the State Archives from a flash flood in the state office building. I found all the Kauai territorial park's correspondence in the bottom of an old Del Monte pineapple carton. Each bit of history that I uncovered was a discovery, and I was quickly caught up in the search for more. I had not known Hawaiians were afraid of the forest or that they had no real conservation tradition, until I researched old manuscripts. I did not know that state personnel in later years had themselves unsuccessfully opposed installation of military radar in Koke'e State Park, until I found corroborative interoffice memos buried deep in their files.

Jim Ferry, then chairman of the State Board of Land and Natural Resources, granted permission for me to search Land Office vaults and files of Forestry, Fish and Game, and Parks. Original government sources were particularly valuable in supplying facts on land management policies of the monarchy, republic, territory and state. Amfac spent a full day searching early corporate records of Kekaha Sugar Company so my chronological history would be in order. Agnes Conrad, in charge of the State Archives, also rendered invaluable assistance in locating old reports and official correspondence. And I must not forget Jean Holmes editor of *The Garden Island*, the capable staff at Kauai Museum and Kauai Public Library. Of considerable assistance was Carol Ann Davis, Kauai Community Arts Coordinator for the State Foundation of Culture and the Arts.

One of my most helpful friends is a camping companion of many years with the Hawaiian Trail and Mountain Club, Richard Davis. Dick sometimes carried more than 50 pounds of my camera gear and tripod on his back, helping me into wilderness back country and moving me up precipitous pali with rope and piton. On one occasion, we were both instantly lost when our helicopter pilot dropped us off in the middle of Alaka'i swamp and we neglected to ask the pilot where we were! We were four days hiking out to the bottom of Waimea canyon.

Alfred Preis first suggested I set down on paper my thoughts on the Hawaiian environment. He is a familiar name to all who have worked to preserve Hawaii's scenic resources, and is now director of the State Foundation for Culture and the Arts. I earlier had worked as a designing draftsman in Preis' Honolulu architectural office. It was a time I'm sure he remembers as more talking than working, but his concern about the islander's relationship to the environment became an important part of my life.

Many Kamaa'ina residents of Kauai graciously granted interviews for my book, and I heard from them bits of Kauai's history I could not have known otherwise. Especially helpful were Mr. and Mrs. Hector Moir, who greeted me with generous hospitality at their Poipu residence a decade ago. It is now a tourist restaurant. They directed me to numerous sources of information, out-of-print publications and family letters from another century. Selwyn Robinson and Alan Faye, both scions of kama'ina families, told me much about early days in Kalalau, Koke'e and Kekaha.

I owe much to Governor John A. Burns, who appointed me a member of the State Land Use Commission during his first administration. As a land use commissioner, I learned of the importance of every vote, and as a political and environmental activist in the sixties I learned how vital it was for the public to be informed about our land environment and the uniqueness of our natural scenic resources. It was my opinion that an informed citizenry would oppose any threat to the scenic beauty that is so much a part of their island lifestyle, and it was my intention to publish photographs and words capable of informing and arousing a concerned public. Politicians would respond accordingly.

Dave Brower, then executive director of the Sierra Club and now president of the Friends of the Earth, provided the opportunity to write and photograph the original version of this book for the Sierra Club, as part of his award-winning exhibit-format series of photographic books. Published in 1967, *Kauai and the Park Country of Hawaii*, edited by Ken Brower, was my first book and its proposal, a great Kauai National Park, was defeated by the ranchers and planters of Kauai opposed to federal regulation of island lands.

This new edition of *Kauai* is my eighth large format photographic book, a series of my own inspired by Dave's first decision that I should, myself, photograph and write *Kauai*. He said I knew best what to say—why tell someone else what to write. After publication, a Smithsonian scientist referred to *Kauai* as, "a masterpiece of popular ecology." It was fortunate that Dave did not ask that I write a book about the ecology of an island. I would have failed.

The Kauai of 1979 is very different from the plantation community of 12 years ago. Kauai today is an active community with a concerned citizenry dedicated to preserving and protecting their unique island environment. It is to the people of Kauai, who love their island as I do, that I owe my greatest acknowledgment.

R. Wenkam

The cliffs of Waimea canyon are the gateway to inner Kauai.

(Overleaf). Possibly the most beautiful beach shore in the Pacific, Lumaha'i-Waikoko shimmers invitingly in the morning sun along Kauai's north shore.

Genesis

Lines from a Hawaiian creation chant

At the time when the earth became hot
At the time when the heavens turned about
At the time when the sun was darkened
To cause the moon to shine
The time of the rise of the Pleiades
The slime, this was the source of the earth
The source of the darkness that made darkness
The source of the night that made night
The intense darkness, the deep darkness
Darkness of the sun, darkness of the night
   Nothing but night

The coral reef at Ha'ena-Ke'e is revealed in a swirling meeting of the sea and shore.

The night gave birth

Born was Kumulipo in the night, a male

Born was Po'ele in the night, a female

Born was the coral polyp, born was the coral, came forth

Born was the grub that digs and heaps up the earth,
came forth

Born was his child an earthworm, came forth

Born was the starfish, his child the small starfish
came forth

Born was the sea cucumber, his child the small sea
cucumber came forth

Born was the sea urchin, the sea urchin tribe

Born was the short-spiked sea urchin, came forth

Born was the smooth sea urchin, his child the long-
spiked came forth

Born was the ring-shaped sea urchin, his child the
thin-spiked came forth

Born was the barnacle, his child the pearl oyster came
forth

Born was the mother-of-pearl, his child the oyster
came forth

Born was the mussel, his child the hermit crab came
forth

Born was the big limpet, his child the small limpet
came forth

Born was the cowry, his child the small cowry
came forth

Born was the naka shellfish, the rock oyster his
child came forth

Born was the drupa shellfish, his child the bitter
white shellfish came forth

Born was the conch shell, his child the small conch
shell came forth

Born was the nerita shellfish, the sand-burrowing
shellfish his child came forth

Born was the fresh-water shellfish, his child the small
fresh-water shellfish came forth

Edible opihi shellfish on the rocky shore of Nu'alolo-'aina.

Out from the slime come rootlets
Out from the slime comes young growth
Out from the slime come branching leaves
Out from the slime comes outgrowth

The native 'ama'u fern thrives in the perpetual dampness of Alaka'i swamp.

Born was man for the narrow stream, the woman for the broad stream
Born was the ekaha moss living in the sea
Guarded by the ekahakaha fern living on land
Darkness slips into light
Earth and water are the food of the plant
The god enters, man cannot enter
Man for the narrow stream, woman for the broad stream
Born was the tough sea-grass living in the sea
Guarded by the tough land-grass living on land

Grassy sedge marks a firm place to step in the Alaka'i bog. The marsh water is stained
tea-brown by the 'ama'u fern.

Born was the egg, the parent
Out came its child a bird, and flew
Born was the Snipe, the parent
Out came its child a Plover, and flew
Born was the A'o bird, the parent
Out came its child an A'u bird, and flew
Born was the Turnstone, the parent
Out came its child a Fly-catcher, and flew
Born was the Mudhen, the parent
Out came its child an Apapane bird, and flew
Born was the Crow, the parent
Out came its child an Alawi bird, and flew
Born was the 'E'ea bird, the parent
Out came its child an Alaaiaha bird, and flew
Born was the Mamo honey-sucker, the parent
Out came its child an 'O'o bird, and flew
Born was the Rail, the parent
Out came its child a brown Albatross, and flew
Born was the Akikiki creeper, the parent
Out came its child an Ukihi bird, and flew
Born was the Curlew, the parent
Out came its child a Stilt, and flew
Born was the Frigate bird, the parent
Out came its child a Tropic bird, and flew
Born was the migrating gray-backed Tern, the parent
Out came its child a red-tailed Tropic-bird, and flew
Born was the Unana bird, the parent
Its offspring the Heron came out and flew
   Flew hither in flocks
   On the seashore in ranks
   Settled down and covered the beach...

Lichen grows slowly upon a volcanic boulder on the beach of Kalalau.

Land birds were born
Sea birds were born
Man born for the narrow stream, woman for the broad stream
Born was the Stingray, living in the sea
Guarded by the Stormy-petrel living on land
Man for the narrow stream, woman for the broad stream
Born was the Sea-swallow, living at sea
Guarded by the hawk living on land

Nothing but darkness that
Nothing but darkness this
Darkness alone for Po'ele'ele
Still it is night

The end of the beach at Kalalau, beyond the end of Napali trail.

The night gives birth to prolific ones
The night is swollen with plump creatures
The night gives birth to rough-backed turtles
The night produces horn-billed turtles
The night gives birth to dark-red turtles
The night is pregnant with the small lobster
The night gives birth to sluggish-moving geckos
Slippery is the night with sleek-skinned geckos
The night gives birth to clinging creatures
The night proclaims rough ones
The night gives birth to deliberate creatures
The night shrinks from the ineffective
The night gives birth to sharpnosed creatures
Hollowed is the night for great fat ones
The night gives birth to mud dwellers
The night lingers for track leavers
Born is the male for the narrow stream, the female for the
broad stream
Born is the turtle (Honu) living in the sea
Guarded by the Maile seedling (Kuhonua) living on land

Man for the narrow steam, woman for the broad stream
Born is the sea-borer (Wili) living in the sea
Guarded by the Wiliwili tree living on land

Man for the narrow stream, woman for the broad stream
Born is the sea-worm living in the sea
Guarded by the bastard sandalwood living on land

Man for the narrow stream, woman for the broad stream
Born is the Okea living in the sea
Guarded by the Ahakea tree living on land

Man for the narrow stream, woman for the broad stream
Born is the sea-urchin (Wana) living in the sea
Guarded by the thorny Wanawana plant living on land

Man for the narrow steam, woman for the broad stream
Born is the Nene shellfish living in the sea
Guarded by the Manene grass living on land

Man for the narrow stream, woman for the broad stream
Born is the Liko living in the sea
Guarded by the Piko tree living on land

Man for the narrow stream, woman for the broad stream
Born is the Opeope jellyfish living in the sea
Guarded by the Oheohe (bamboo) living on land

Man for the narrow stream, woman for the broad stream
Born is the Nanana (sea spider) living in the sea
Guarded by the Nonanona living on land

Born was Pola'a
Born was rough weather, born the current
Born the booming of the sea, the breaking of foam
Born the roaring, advancing, and receding of waves,
. .the rumbling sound, the earthquake
The sea rages, rises over the beach
Rises silently to the inhabited places
Rises gradually up over the land

Coral limestone roughens the ocean waves of Maha'ulepu beyond Koloa.

Born is the stormy night
Born the night of plenty...
Dead is the current sweeping in from the navel of the
..earth: that was a warrior wave
Many who came vanished, lost in the passing night

Born were men by the hundreds
Born was man for the narrow stream
Born was woman for the broad stream
Born the night of the gods
Men stood together
Men slept together
They two slept together in the time long ago
Wave after wave of men moving in company...
Tranquil was the time when men multiplied
Calm like the time when men came from afar
It was called Calmness (La 'ila'i) then
Born was La'ila'i a woman
Born was Ki'i a man
Born was Kane a god..

Born was Kanaloa the hot-striking octopus...
Born was Creeping-ti-plant (La'i'olo) to man
Born was Expected-day (Kapopo), a female
Born was Midnight (Po'ele-i), born First-light (Po'ele-a)
Opening-wide (Wehi-loa) was their youngest
These were those who gave birth
The little ones, the older ones
Ever increasing in number
Man spread abroad, man was here now
It was Day.

The Kumulipo
—translated by Martha Beckwith

Vines of Morning Glory spread across the dunes of Barking Sands.

Kalalau Valley

Kauai is Discovered for the Second Time

Toward the end of the eighteenth century Hawaii was discovered for the second time in nine hundred years. The first discovery, by Polynesians, had changed the land little, but the second discovery was by a different sort of traveler.

IN THE WINTER of 1777-78, Captain James Cook sailed north from Christmas Island for five weeks, searching for a northwest passage. On February 1, he wrote in his log:

"The wind shifted, and a storm came on, preceded by a lowering darkness, that prefaced some violent convulsion, and soon after it broke forth in thunder, lightening, wind, and rain, which in two hours increased to such a raging degree, as no man on board had ever known the like. Fortunately, it was but of short continuance; but, in that little time, the sea broke over our quarter, and cleared the decks of everything that was loose. After this we had a gentle breeze an east and east southeast which continued till we arrive in the latitude of 7 deg. 45 min. north and in 205 deg. east longitude, where we had one day of perfect calm. A northeast by east wind then succeeded, which blew faintly at first, but freshened as we proceeded northward. We daily observed tropic birds, boobies, etc. and between the latitude of 10 and 11 deg. north we saw several turtles. Though all these are considered as signs of the proximity of land, we discovered none till early in the morning of Sunday, the 18th, when an island appeared bearing northeast by east not long after more land was seen, which bore north and was totally detached from the former. At noon, the first was supposed to be 8 or 9 leagues distant. Our longitude at this time, was 200 deg. 41 min. east and our latitude 21 deg. 12 min. north. The next day, at sunrise, the island first seen bore east distant 7 leagues, not being able to reach this, we shaped our course for the other; and soon after, observed a third island, bearing west northwest. We had now a fine breeze at east by north and, at noon, the second island…for the east end of which we were steering, was about two leagues distant. As we made a nearer approach, many of the inhabitants put off from the shore in their canoes, and very readily came alongside the ships."

Captain Cook put ashore at Waimea and looked from the sea to the wooded mountains of this strange land he named in honor of the Earl of Sandwich. He noted only "grass tuffs, not even shrubs," where he landed. The lower part of the country was treeless. He saw few coconuts, only a rare breadfruit, and "houses scattered about without any order."

Cook compared Hawaii unfavorably with Tahiti, but found on Kauai "a greater quantity of gently-rising land, (which) renders it, in some measure, superior to the above favourite islands, as being more capable of development."

For seven years after Cook's departure, no foreigner set foot on Kauai, until Captain Vancouver came. Vancouver presented to a Waimea Chief the first sheep and horned cattle ever seen in the islands. He also gave to one of the chiefs "some vine and orange plants, some almonds, and an assortment of garden seeds."

The discovery of the islands of Hawaii opened up new lands for foreign businessmen, who sailed from Europe and America.

Fortune-hunters joined conservative financiers in acquiring land on all the islands—legally or otherwise. The Hawaiian civilization was corrupted by American business in an era of great disappointment to frustrated missionaries. King Kalakaua, in a poker game, showed the mood of the times. The King, playing with Maui sugar baron Claus Spreckels, said, "I have four kings," placing on the felt table top his hand of three kings and pointing to himself as the fourth.

The Monarchy's objective of increasing the Islands' export revenues led to the support of a single-use land policy and a plantation system of efficient land utilization. Little attempt was made to encourage homesteading or to establish family farms. Most of the valuable lands suitable for large-scale agriculture, much of the beach land, and the desirable urban areas were quickly acquired through widespread grants to large plantations and private estates. With few exceptions, most of the public lands were marginal acreage: swamplands, eroded pasture, and inaccessible mountain lands.

The Hawaiian native population was dropping alarmingly and land was plentiful. Mark Twain visited Hawaii and reported:

"The natives of the islands number only about 50,000 and the whites about 3,000, chiefly Americans. According to Capt. Cook, the natives numbered 400,000 less than a hundred years ago. But the traders brought labor and fancy diseases—in other words, long, deliberate, infallible destruction; and the missionaries brought the means of grace and got them ready. So the two forces are working along harmoniously, and anybody who knows anything about figures can tell you exactly when the last Kanaka will be in Abraham's bosom and his islands in the hands of the whites. It is the same as calculating an eclipse—if you get started right, you cannot miss it. For nearly a century the natives have been keeping up a ratio of about three births to five deaths, and you can see what that must result in. No doubt in fifty years a Kanaka will be a curiosity in his own land, and as an investment will be superior to a circus."

THE FEW REMAINING forests diminished as great sugar plantations spread across the land. A koa tree at that time, as an investment, would have been superior to a circus—except that no one was interested in seeing a *koa*, and certainly not in paying admission.

Forests receded, and the barren fields of dry, red earth at Makaweli fed giant dust clouds. Red dust, carried by trade winds, blew miles out to sea from Waimea and Kehaha. For days at a time during trade-wind weather, ships could not see the harbor and were forced to wait offshore.

The land was changing, but industry was prospering. In a few decades Hawaii was to boast the largest sugar plantation, the largest fruit farm (pineapples), and the second largest cattle ranch in the United States. □

Kauai floats alone in the island chain.

Sugar Transforms an Island Eden

The Eden the Hawaiians had known was transformed. Sugar became the most important force in the islands, and its cultivation had an unparalleled impact on the Hawaiian landscape. The industry had slow and difficult beginnings, dependent upon the dedication of the pioneer planters, men who worked hard, risked much, and often lost.

VALDEMAR KNUDSEN arrived in Hawaii in April 1854, from California's Feather River country, with little experience in ranching or agriculture. He took an early liking to the warm west shore beyond Waimea, and gratefully took up the offer of his friend, ranch-owner H. A. Widemann, to tend several dozen head of cattle. Knudsen was able to fatten the cattle quickly on the warm Kekaha grasslands, and acquired valuable experience in ranching operations. The aggressive and sensitive young bachelor quickly adopted Hawaii as home, learned the Hawaiian language, and soon gained the friendship and confidence of both native chiefs and commoners.

A contemporary of Knudsen, Archibald Archer, was the first white farmer of Kekaha. He grew oranges, coffee, and tobacco in Hanalei Valley, and cleared ground for tobacco in Mana. Hoping for better growing weather, Archer sought and was granted the first Crown lease in west Kauai, yet continued to plant in Hanalei, hiking there across the vast wet top of Kauai in two days, following old Hawaiian trails. He built a small grass hut at Halemanu to rest overnight on his incredible journeys up Mana Ridge on horseback, across Alakai Swamp to Kilohana on foot, and down the almost vertical palis of Wainiha Valley. After holding the lease for five years, he lost everything following an extended drought. Then his partner died. Discouraged, he sailed away after reaching an agreement to have Knudsen take over the lease.

Knudsen negotiated a new thirty-year lease with King Kamehameha's commissioners of public lands. For an annual rental of four thousand dollars in U.S. gold coin, he signed the lease for all commercial rights to "those tracts of land situated at Waimea, island of Kauai, Hawaiian Islands, known as the Ahupua'a of Kekaha, Poki'i, Waiawa, Mokihana, Miloli'i, Nu'alolo, and Mana, by their ancient boundaries...subject however to the legal rights of native tenants."

In addition to the usual lease conditions and clauses covering reversion of improvements to the kingdom, the Crown's indenture included a new lease condition reflecting concern by the King over the depredation of his forests for sandalwood and the increasing damage from wild cattle. The lessee was admonished not to "permit or suffer to be done, any willful or voluntary waste, spoil or destruction...upon the above demised premises, or cut down, or permit to be cut down any timber trees now growing or which shall hereafter grow..."

Knudsen built his home at Waiawa on the edge of Mana Swamp. At that time the great swamp covered large areas of the lowlands and its connected brackish lakes allowed natives from Mana Village to paddle on an inland sea as far as Waimea. Migratory ducks flying the Pacific on their southern route fed on the swamp plants. Thousands of cranelike Hawaiian stilts stood on spindly pink legs in the still swamp waters. Dunes rippled along the coral limestone shoreline and protected the lakes from high seas and salt water.

The high plateau behind Knudsen's home was blanketed by a dense and luxuriant forest of indigenous ohi'a lehua, and koa. The abundant birds, of varieties he had never seen before, Knudsen carefully collected and sent to Washington. One skin—that of the Hawaiian stilt—was new to the Smithsonian Institution scientists, who named the bird after its finder: *Himantopus himanptopus Knudseni*. The Hawaiians simply called it Ae'o.

When Knudsen signed the Waimea lease, he became a *konohiki*, or chief, by appointment of Kamehameha IV. In this office he possessed princely powers over a district that covered more than one hundred square miles—almost all the west side of Kauai from the sandy shore at Mana to the high Waineke pond of Kokee and beyond to Napali.

Hundreds of natives were scattered through the district, living in grass huts and tending taro patches that had been in continuous use since ancient days. Knudsen spoke to them in Hawaiian and received their loyalty. They called him Kanuka. He was the *Alii O Kauai*, the Lord of Kauai.

KNUDSEN LIVED in a time of bold transition: transition from ancient native tenancy to modern leasehold, from the absolute powers of the *Konohiki* to those of the landlord.

Before Knudsen's coming, in 1840, the new constitutional monarchy had proclaimed revised labor-tax laws as a first step in reforming the feudal kingdom of King Kamehameha. The new laws provided that the commoner would no longer be required to work for the king and chiefs on every week of the month: "the first week of the month the people shall work two days for the king and one for the landlords, the second week in the month they shall work one day for his Majesty, the King, and two days for the landlords, and the next two weeks the people shall have to themselves."

The annual royal tax was in accordance with a regular system, assessed on the smallest divisions of land, and was paid somewhat as follows: one 'ili (individual parcel) was "taxed a hog, a

Waimea Canyon, where the earth and weather meet.

dog, a fish net, a fish line, a cluster of feathers, and 20 kapas (tapa cloths)." Some of the kapas were to be nearly square, for bed clothes, and some narrow and long for women's dresses.

The new laws also provided for a redistribution of the fishing grounds. Waters outside of coral reefs were assigned to the commoner; those between reefs and beach, to landlords. Certain specified grounds and species of fish were "placed under the protective kapu of the tax officers for the king." Sandalwood trees, the 'o'o and mamo birds, and "all large trees such as one cannot clasp" were kapu, and violation was punished by a fine of "one hundred rafters each five yards long." The beach was unassigned and available to all. To this day, the beach between the high water mark and the sea remains reserved for public use.

The foundation for the Monarchy's land reform had been laid long before. By the time Captain Cook arrived on Kauai, the Hawaiians had already established land divisions on the separate islands for easier control and tax collecting. Each island was divided into districts called "moku." The large moku was divided into long pie-shaped parcels that extended from the mountains to the sea, and were called "ahupua'a." Managed by konohiki, these unique land divisions enabled commoners living on the ahupua'a within their chief's authority to satisfy the tax collector without trespassing on ahupua'a of adjacent chiefs. Fish and seaweed were obtained from the sea; taro, bananas, and sweet potatoes from the lowlands; and feathers, canoe logs, and spears from the mountains. Ahupua'a varied greatly in size and were sometimes cut off from access to the sea or mountains by the odd shapes of other ahupua'a, but their primary purpose of providing for all a man's needs was an unusual characteristic for a political land division.

Smaller units within the ahupua'a were 'ili, each with its own name and carefully defined boundary. Sometimes an 'ili was divided and its parts separated. The natives called this kind of 'ili a lele, the Hawaiian word for jump.

THE CULTIVATED portions of the 'ili were subdivided further into small tracts of land called mo'o or mo'o'aina. Occasionally a mo'o was subdivided again into smaller parcels called pauka. The commoners facilitated tax payments by cultivating still smaller plots which were worked on the "chief's day." Since these patches were generally worked only on Friday, they became known as po'alima, Fridays. The native's own small farming patch, which he tilled for himself was called a kihapai.

The single most important land reform by the Hawaiian Monarchy was the Great Mahele—the Great Division—of 1848. Its proclamation by King Kamehameha III opened the way for private ownership of land. In the Great Mahele the land interests of the king and high-ranking chiefs were divided among the people in a momentous undertaking of far-reaching consequences.

In 1845, a Land Commission had been appointed by King Kamehameha III to determine the rights of all individuals to their claim in the land, whether they were chiefs or commoners. The Land Commission, in carrying out its work, had recommended division of all lands into three parts: the king's personal property, the land of the chiefs and konohiki, and the land being tenanted by the common people. The Mahele made no provision for

ownership of land by the tenant Hawaiians, although a bill of rights did protect them from unwarranted dispossession.

The king and chiefs strongly objected to the idea of distributing their land, but they yielded to pressure from the sugar planters and the realization that the economy of the islands would suffer unless the old feudal system was abandoned. More than two hundred and forty of the highest ranking chiefs and konohiki participated. The individual divisions were recorded in a huge book called the "Mahele book," with lands signed over to the chiefs listed on the right side and lands reserved for the king on the left. The Mahele was made without any survey, the land being identified by its ancient name and described in the Mahele book by natural geographic features, a mountain ridge or the bottom of a gulch, and sometimes merely by a field of grass, the stone walls of taro patches, or a particularly large and significant tree. The descriptions of early land divisions still plague surveyors, and many carefully described parcels are today lost in plowed and featureless caneland.

THE KING'S PERSONAL properties were called The Crown Lands, and the lands of the chiefs and people were called Government Lands. Government Lands were leased or sold from time to time as a means of obtaining revenue to meet the increasingly high costs of the government and to satisfy the demands of the sugar planters and ranchers for large landholdings.

As the king and chiefs began to dispose of their newly acquired holdings, many questions arose regarding the rights of native tenants. To clarify the situation, the privy council authorized the land commission to award fee simple titles to all native tenants without payment, finally allowing the commoner to own his own land. These parcels of various shapes and sizes became known as "Kuleana Lands" and today are proudly owned by the few Hawaiians still living on the land.

It was necessary for the native tenant to file legal claims for his kuleana, but many thousands failed to register or to appear before the Land Commission in support of their claims. Of the approximately 4,000,000 acres of land divided in the Great Mahele of 1848, only 30,000 acres of land were awarded to native Hawaiian commoners; these were mostly taro lands, at the time considered the most valuable lands in the islands.

Few Hawaiians understood the new land laws, and the isolated natives of Niihau Island were not alone in failing to register the land their fathers and ancestors had lived on for generations. On Niihau only one parcel was recorded with the king's appointed registrars.

Niihau was one of several grants of land offered to the Sinclair family by King Kamehameha V. The island stood across the channel from Waimea, fifteen miles from Kauai. Francis Sinclair, who liked the idea of owning his own island, convinced the family of Niihau's potential as a ranch, and in 1864 they paid the king ten thousand dollars for sole ownership. The family moved to Niihau, where they immediately found their newly purchased authority as landlords challenged by the native Hawaiians, who had no understanding or respect for private land ownership. The land had always been theirs to grow crops on and hunt as they needed to feed and clothe their families. Their only obligation

had been to the Hawaiian chiefs who received a share of the yams and an occasional pig.

Sinclair's revival of the old feudal rental system and his refusal to recognize Hawaiian ownership of kuleana the Hawaiians had neglected to legalize generated ill will among the Hawaiians and destroyed the Sinclairs' dream of an island paradise. Sinclair demanded one or more day's labor a month in exchange for rights to live and hunt on Niihau. Many natives refused to comply and few had any desire to hire out as ranch hands. Fish were plentiful in the sea and taro was easily available from Kauai. Sweet potatoes and yams grew alongside their grass huts and coconuts loaded the palms overhead. Working for the Sinclair family appeared to offer nothing they did not already have in abundance.

RANCHING OPERATIONS virtually stopped when one elderly Hawaiian couple refused to allow cowboys to graze cattle across their *kuleana* or even to set foot upon the land they claimed for their own. The disputed strip of land reached from the mountains to the sea, and cut off all travel from one end of the island to the other. The Sinclairs were dumbfounded when proof was offered that 50 acres of land on Niihau had indeed been granted to a Hawaiian named Papapa by King Kamehameha III in 1855, nine years before the Sinclairs' purchase. The king in selling Niihau apparently overlooked the earlier grant, and the new owners were now challenged by two hostile Hawaiians who refused to allow them even a right-of-way across the narrow parcel.

Francis Sinclair discussed his problem with Valdemar Knudsen, konohiki of western Kauai. Sinclair was willing to pay one thousand dollars for the land, though the entire island had sold for only ten thousand. Knudsen was held in high respect by the Hawaiians in his ahupua'a. He agreed to negotiate with the Papapa couple and asked Sinclair to bring him one thousand silver dollars.

Arriving on Niihau by longboat, Knudsen traveled overland on horseback to the Papapa' grass hut on the western shore, and introduced himself. As he talked with the old couple, he carefully stacked the silver dollars in orderly rows across the lauhala mat spread over the floor. The old man kept shaking his head "no," emphasizing again and again his unwillingness to sell. Knudsen continued to stack the silver coins, telling the couple of the new merchants on Kauai, where the land was gentler and greener, and where they could enjoy their remaining days without ever working again. The piles of coins, ten to a stack, grew on the mat. The old man repeated no, as his wife's eyes opened wide in wonder. She listened silently. At last Knudsen shrugged and began unstacking the coins. Suddenly, the wife uttered an ancient Hawaiian exclamation, "Schah!," reached out, and pulled the treasure into her lap. The Sinclairs at last owned all Niihau.

The Sinclairs soon became aware that Niihau was useless as a profitable ranch, and purchased Makaweli grant, probably the most valuable single parcel on Kauai, stretching from Waimea River to Olokele and Hanapepe, from Wai'ale'ale to the sea. By 1957 the family's lands on Kauai and Niihau totaled 97,291 acres with an estimated market value of $4,971,000. Niihau's 46,000 acres were worth only $190,000.

As pioneering traders and merchants began to seek fortunes in cattle and sugar, the problems experienced by the Sinclairs on Niihau became commonplace across the land. Communications with the king were very unreliable, and it was not in the best interests of the chiefs to proclaim the new rights granted to the commoners in a way that all would understand.

Valdemar Knudsen escaped much of this trouble. He understood the Hawaiians and was almost as undemanding as they were in his relationship with the land. He was a poor businessman and an undedicated farmer. He experimented freely with his land, importing plants from many countries. Visiting botanists from all over the world were his house guests, and many responded to his hospitality with gifts of fruit and flower seeds. Knudsen's Waiawa property blossomed with trees and vines from far lands. He brought in the first kiawe tree seeds to Kauai from Honolulu's Catholic mission; his cattle were to fatten contentedly on the ripe seed pods in later years during the long, hot Kekaha summers. The swamps with his beloved birds remained undisturbed, and he urged the king to protect Nohili, Kawalele, and Kolo ponds at Mana as game preserves.

When Knudsen and Dora Isenberg, wife of the German manager of Lihue Plantation, received packets of koa haole seeds, Knudsen planted his near Waiawa, from where they soon spread to all sections of the island. The koa haole plants provided excellent cattle feed, but were to become an unsightly pest. Dora Isenberg remarked later that "You can blame Valdemar for koa haole—I flushed mine down the toilet!" Winds blew the flat brown seed everywhere.

KNUDSEN RANGED FAR and wide on his favorite horse, Pukuniahi, planting orange trees in every gulch piercing the Mana Pali, where they grew rapidly and flourished. When the bachelor Knudsen courted and received the hand of Annie Sinclair, he gathered his own orange blossoms and carried the fragrant bouquet to his bride. They settled down quietly to live on his adopted land.

Captain Christian L'Orange, a sailor who left his ship in Honolulu to make a fortune on the land, formed a partnership with Knudsen. They planted the first commercial sugar cane in the Kekaha area at Poki'i in 1878. Knudsen improved the small spring at Kauhika with a steam pump and hired natives at fifty cents a day to plant cane and harvest the crop. When the Hawaiians tired of working for wages and went fishing, the partners sold out to two other planters who were willing to take over.

Knudsen returned to his ranch, boiled down wild cattle for tallow, bailed hides, and sold salted meat to whalers. The high mountain country provided ideal pasturage for breeding the bullocks that hauled the large bull-carts, piled high with handcut sugar cane, to the new cane-grinding mill at Kekaha. Paying the annual land rental proved difficult until Knudsen's subleases for sugar cane began earning a regular income. Knudsen was often forced to pay the rental with taro, firewood, breadfruit, and pigs brought to him by the natives on his orders as the konohiki of Waimea and West Kauai.

It was a frontier life for the Knudsens. Henry Restarick, the Bishop of Honolulu, visited the family when they were well

Beyond Mana the dry sands bark when walked upon. Polihale is the westernmost limit of Napali.

established at Waiawa, and later described his trip.

I was to be the guest of the Knudsens at Kekaha, and I shall never forget the ride from Ele'ele to their home. It was before the great improvement was made in the roads and the red dust was deep, impalpable and penetrating. A bath with three changes of water did not eliminate it from the pores of my skin, or my hair, and my hosts, the Knudsens, laughed when, like David Harum, I apologized for the state of the towels. They comforted me by saying that when I reached home my pillows would show for weeks where I had been. I have since heard the story of the Kauai man who made a journey round the world, and on reaching San Francisco, on his way home, he took a Turkish bath. When he was rubbed down the man said, "you are from Kauai, sir." "How do you know?" "I can tell from the color of the dirt. I was there once myself."

KNUDSEN'S NEPHEW from Norway, Hans P. Faye, joined the small group of cane planters in later years. It was he who drilled the first artesian well near Waiawa. Cane grew rapidly in the warm sunshine and plentiful water, attracting new investors and planters from all sections of Kauai. A Chinese merchant, Pah On, built a rice mill at Waimea and harvested rice at Mana in quantities sufficient to supply all the islands until the Sacramento delta was planted, making his venture unprofitable in competition with cheaper California rice.

The Hawaiians could not be persuaded to work on the plantations, and it became necessary to import Portuguese, Chinese, and Japanese as contract laborers. Discouraged by what he felt was the failure of his Hawaiians, and aging, Knudsen became seriously ill from a recurring fever and disappeared for months at a time, leaving Annie to care for the children and manage the lands, with help from her brother Frank on Niihau. Paul Isenberg convinced Annie that she should sign over all the sugar-growing lands to a new planters' company he organized, which would harvest the cane and divide the profits between themselves and Annie. She agreed, keeping their home at Waiawa and the grazing land above the Mana Pali. The new sugar firm, Kekaha Sugar Company, prospered and paid Annie's share of profits in raw sugar, bagged and warehoused in her name.

In July 1918, Knudsen's sons, Eric and Augustus, upon advice that the sugar enterprise was a risky business, sold the remaining term of Valdemar Knudsen's lease to Kekaha Sugar Company. Eighteen months remained of the thirty-year lease that was paying Annie eighty thousand dollars a year for government land leasing at four thousand. Fortunes were handsomely made in sugar and Kekaha was no exception.

Valdemar Knudsen died in Honolulu in 1898. He helped plant the seeds of a growing industry with powerful political influence, an industry that history credits with overthrowing the monarchy and bringing about annexation of Hawaii to the United States. As the sugar industry prospered, the Hawaiian culture dwindled, and the vigor and glory of the race disappeared. The native grass-hut villages and taro patches were replaced by a new civilization and land wrapped in a green carpet of sugar.☐

ROBERT WENKAM has much in common with Valdemar Knudsen, the early planter whose story he tells here. Though their arrivals were a century apart, both men fell in love with Hawaii and adopted the islands as home. Their love was not the love typical of newcomers to Hawaii; they were not much enamoured of the rich soil and what it might produce, or of the pleasant climate, or of the beaches. They were not excited by the potential of Hawaii, but by what Hawaii was—by the land itself and what was native to it. The two ranged their adoptive country widely, a century apart, the earlier arrival on his horse, the later on his very long legs.

Both Wenkam and Knudsen arrived as young men, unsure at the direction their lives would take. For both, the Hawaiian land made the decision—a healthy way to have one's destiny shaped. Knudsen became a sometime farmer and Hawaiian chief. Wenkam became a photographer and a conservationist, the leader of the fight for a national park on Kauai.

The country of western Kauai would make a unique national park. Its forests are like no other forests in our national park system, and its sea cliffs like no other cliffs. There are birds and plants there found nowhere else, last Hawaiian examples of the local modification that makes islands so interesting to evolutionists. Best of all, there are the *menehune*, the tiny forest people who came to Hawaii before the Polynesians and are still in the deep forest, according to Hawaiians who should know. (Recently a class on Kauai was disrupted when one of the children saw a menehune by a well. The teacher joined in the hunt, which continued until the principal arrived.)

No present national park boasts supernatural beings, not Yellowstone nor Yosemite nor Grand Canyon. Here, then, is the chance for a truly unique national park, and Wenkam saw it—the opportunity to make an invaluable addition to our nearly perfect park system.

— Ken Brower

Erosion scars on Kalalau valley's pali talus exposes Kauai's famous red dirt.

Sugar and Hawaiians—Land and Politics

*Sugar interests dominated island politics and their
right to do as they pleased with the land was
unquestioned. No voice spoke for the integrity of the
land, and the land suffered*

THE COURSE of public land use following the Great Mahele is well illustrated in the history of lands occupied by Kauai's Kekaha Sugar Company. Kekaha's history is a part in the story of how a government-sponsored land monopoly determined not only the economy of the islands, but also the very mood and appearance of the land.

Outright purchase of large land grants by the plantations had been stopped long before Kekaha Sugar was founded. The Kingdom's policy of leasing lands instead of selling them had been initiated in order to halt the rapidly dwindling public domain. Later, the United States Congress, in writing the organic act establishing the Territory of Hawaii, included provisions that protected Hawaiians from being stripped of their land heritage, and the leasing policy was continued for that purpose.

Kekaha began its corporate history as the only plantation completely on government-leased land. Businessmen of the time must have raised their eyebrows as Kekaha cleared land, planted cane, and constructed a grinding mill at great cost, all with only a fifteen-year lease. The venture proved quite profitable, however.

As Kekaha's first lease renewal time approached, plantation manager Hans P. Faye became concerned when the new Territory of Hawaii asserted that upon termination of the lease expensive mill machinery would revert to the government, in addition to buildings, irrigation ditches, and other improvements. Faye disagreed with the Territory, and in a letter to C.T. Bailey, Commissioner of Public Lands, offered $150,000 to buy the land around mill and plantation improvements, pleading that he could not make needed mill improvements without full ownership. Without objecting, Commissioner Bailey deleted the 40-acre mill site from Kekaha's 28,000-acre master lease, and following the provisions of the organic act, placed the land on the auction block for the competitive bidding that had to occur before land was leased. March 13, 1922 was the day of the auction. Only two Honolulu men registered to bid: W.T. Bottomley, acting as agent for Kekaha, and his close friend, E. White Sutton of Bishop Trust Company. The auction took only a few minutes. The short-term leases on pastures and rice fields went to Kekaha at the upset price (the fixed minimum price) of $3,000 annual rental. The fifteen-year sugar-land lease also went for the upset bid of $103,000 plus 7½ per cent of gross sugar receipts. Kekaha had no other bidder for its mill, so the Territory, having agreed that Faye's offer for the forty-acre mill site, camp lands, and improvements was fair and equitable, sold the mill outright to Kekaha in fee simple for $150,000 cash.

The ranch lands brought out curious competitive bidding. Sutton raised the $3,600 upset price by five dollars. Bottomley smiled and raised it another five. "Sold," said the Territorial land agent, and Kekaha acquired the ranch land lease for $3,610.

Competitive bidding had occurred for the first and only time in Kekaha's history.

With factory improvements completed and secured by fee simple ownership of the mill site, manager Faye examined his company's leased acreage closely for new cane lands to feed greater tonnage into his modernized mill. Additional raw sugar could be produced profitably with little increase in overhead. Kekaha could also safely increase planting without fear of losing leasehold lands. Without the mill, Faye correctly reasoned, no one would ever be able to outbid Kekaha, which would obtain every future lease at the upset price. Faye's first move was to gradually phase out the rice growers around the Mana ponds and to replant the paddies in cane.

On August 20, 1925, Faye wrote again to land commissioner Bailey and asked if Kekaha might be able to obtain on lease the Mana game reserves. The Territorial Division of Fish and Game said they "were not interested in creation of a reservation" at Mana, although at the time of the 1922 public auction the lands were specifically excluded from the lease and designated as a game reserve. Knudsen was no longer able to speak for his birds, and the plantation-oriented Territorial Land Department wrote Faye asking him to submit an offer for the 583 acres. This Faye did, and the only remaining migratory bird ponds on Kauai were leased at public auction to Kekaha Sugar for an annual rental of $900, the upset price.

KEKAHA DISPOSSESSED the Hawaiian stilts, the migratory birds, and ducks from their native habitat. The ponds were filled and planted in cane. In 1936, Governor Lucius G. Pinkham's executive order setting aside 550 acres of Mana land for a territorial airport was also canceled. The airport pasture lands were leased to Kekaha, which promptly planted them in cane. The Territory's unwritten policy of promoting a single industry and a single land use was revealing itself as Kekaha expanded rapidly across all available land, eliminating the small farmer and showing little sympathy for conservation concepts encouraging protection of unique flora and fauna. Even Knudsen's old Waiawa home with its view across the Mana ponds to Niihau was dismantled, trees uprooted, and the yards planted in cane.

Chinese and Japanese contract laborers found it difficult to grow vegetables in backyard gardens in Kekaha because of the consistently hot weather, scanty rainfall, and sandy soil. During dry seasons the community was isolated and almost wholly dependent upon mainland importations shipped via Honolulu. Often the workers went without fresh vegetables for weeks at a time. Manager Lindsay Faye responded to their complaints, and 50 acres of marginal land above the mill became a truck-farm

Sugar production in Hawaii is highly mechanized. Only a few field workers are required to operate fleets of equipment, replacing the hundreds of workers loading and cutting cane by hand only fifty years ago.

The sugar mill at Kekaha.

operation with all work done by hand. The operation was successful and soon expanded to 125 acres in a higher area at 2,500 feet, suitable for year-round vegetable growing, along the new Kekaha irrigation ditch bringing water from Alaka'i Swamp. No effort was made to sell outside the community, and Kekaha soon found itself the only company town in the Territory growing its own food and raising its own meat and poultry. Kekaha was entirely self-sufficient.

The second round of fifteen-year lease negotiations opened in 1936 with a letter from H.A. Walker, Honolulu financial agent for Kekaha Sugar Company, proposing new lease terms to the Land Commissioner, suggesting that the annual land rental be computed as a percentage of gross sugar proceeds.

When maverick Kauai Senator Charles A. Rice read Kekaha's proposal, he wrote the new Commissioner of Public Lands, L. M. Whitehouse, a letter that was to postpone the public auction and was perhaps the first direct challenge of Kekaha's land monopoly and long land tenure. The Senator wrote, in words that must have sounded heretical to the sugar planter communities of 1936, that 'The proposition he makes is so unfair to the Government and taxpayers that I request before any action is taken that I be given an opportunity to appear before the Land Board as a Senator from and one who knows the conditions at Kekaha."

Charles Rice ran his own political organization on Kauai and was subservient to no one. He was no longer general manager for American Factors on Kauai and he showed little inclination to recognize old loyalties. He stuck to his principles regarding the Kekaha lease. When Elsie Wilcox of Grove Farm opposed his continued chairmanship of the Senate Ways and Means Committee, Rice retaliated by selling private property in Lihu'e town to Kress Stores and a Japanese merchant, opening up the first competition to the American Factors' company store in Lihu'e. Before Rice's action, no merchant was able to buy land in Lihu'e because almost all the town was owned by Lihu'e Plantation.

The threat to Kekaha's tenure had been raised. Others would soon enter the arena.

FRED PATTERSON, a young Honolulu attorney apparently representing a Los Angeles syndicate, was the first to step forward. He wrote Whitehouse that he wished to bid in the 1938 auction and requested that the Territory provide a new mill site on government land so he could bid competitively against Kekaha. He even offered to build a new mill if he submitted the highest bid. He asked further that a sealed confidential-bid procedure be followed so that Kekaha would be forced to bid higher than the upset price to give a fairer return to the government.

Kekaha had been a profitable enterprise during the old lease. Capital stock was doubled by the issuance of stock dividends amounting to $1,500,000, all of which was directly or indirectly earned from government-leased land. In addition, at the end of 1935 undivided profits totaled $1,422,813. During the thirteen years of the lease, average yearly cash dividends were $397,500 or 27.1 per cent on capital stock. The company had clearly profited beyond all reasonable expectations. The national depression did not affect Kekaha Plantation.

Water rights were publicly owned, as well as the irrigation ditches built by Kekaha Sugar. Without tremendous quantities of water, there would be no sugar—and no profit. Under these conditions it was reasonable to assume that there be a fair division of profits between the company and the Territory.

The Land Department had enough independence to suggest in a memo "that a fair and reasonable rent for the Kekaha lands would be an equitable division of the estimated profits"—a frightening proposal for the government to have made in the ultraconservative Hawaiian business community of 1936.

Early the next year, Senator Rice, who was now Chairman of the Territorial Senate Committee on Public Lands, wrote the assistant to Secretary of Interior Harold Ickes, complaining about the low rentals paid by the sugar plantations. He suggested that homesteaders would be willing to pay more. He wrote, "While I understand that not all of the government land leased to plantations can or should be cut up because of the irrigation and harvesting elements, I believe that at least 100 more of these homesteads could be disposed of on Kauai with a general good effect on the population." He gave as an example lands on eastern Kauai. Here the government lease on sugar lands had not been renewed, and instead had been divided into sixty-one three-acre lots for homesteading and sale at auction.

"As a result of this opportunity, citizens of the Territory now own their own lands and homes, with surrounding gardens. There was spirited bidding at the auction. More than forty of the lots brought more than the upset price."

The leasing of large blocks of government land at low cost to the sugar and ranching industries had long blocked the creation in Hawaii of an independent, farm-owning population, and was described by the 1937 Congressional Statehood Committee as "one of the outstanding evils of Hawaii's present economic setup." Senator Rice agreed.

It was at this time that Governor Joseph Poindexter received a concerned note from the U. S. Department of the Interior which said, 'The decreased income to the Territory is undoubtedly causing an increase in the taxes paid by the people of Hawaii." The governor asked for an investigation. It had become obvious, even in Washington, that government land leases were being manipulated to keep the land available to only a favored few.

This high-level correspondence did not ruffle the Land Commissioner. His office was dedicated to furthering the best interests of Hawaii's fastest growing and most profitable industry. After receiving a letter from Kekaha stating they wanted payment made as originally requested—on a sliding-scale percentage of gross—and would have nothing to do with a division of net proceeds, he asked the Land Board to approve Kekaha's application for a new lease.

The lease application, prepared by C. T. Bailey, former Territorial Land Commissioner and new manager of American Factors' Land Department, was submitted to the Board in October, calling for a new lease at the upset minimum of $130,000 and sliding-scale payments at 7½ per cent of gross proceeds. The Board ignored Senator Rice's objections, unanimously ap-

'Ohi'a lehua growing on the rim of Kalalau.

proved the application, and moved for the auction to be held. As an added measure to make it more difficult for outside bids in the future, Board member Charles Hite, then also Secretary of Hawaii, moved that the power plant and campsite lands of the plantation be sold outright, although they were completely surrounded by Territorial lands. It was in this manner that Kekaha was to acquire in fee simple the powerhouse site deep in the bottom of Waimea Canyon. The legal requirements were met and the cards stacked against any outside bidders for the Kekaha lease.

Pan American's Trans-Pacific China Clipper service brought Hawaii suddenly closer to the mainland, with some new problems for the Land Commissioner. In the fall of 1937 businessman George Rodiek sent a personal letter by clipper mail from San Francisco to Secretary Charles Hite. Rodiek made a lease proposal "which, at all times, would give the landowner 50 per cent of the profits made by the operating company." Rodiek wanted to bid on cane land only, and made an offer on that basis. Whitehouse, apparently attempting to discourage any bidding from outside Hawaii, replied that the new lease rate would have to include all cane and ranch lands, 36,760 acres. This was the difficulty for outsiders anticipated by Bailey when he made his comprehensive bid application.

With the Patterson and Rodiek syndicates seriously interested in bidding, things were becoming complicated for Land Commissioner Whitehouse. Other problems came up. One day he opened a registered airmail letter from Kauai carried by the new interisland airways. It was from Henry K. Aki in Lihu'e, writing for a "blank application for homestead in the island of Kauai." Whitehouse was pleased to answer what he thought to be a routine request and directed Aki to D. F. Hurley, land agent in Lihu'e, who shortly informed Honolulu that Aki wanted many copies and would Whitehouse "please send us a supply."

WHITEHOUSE WROTE Hurley anxiously by return mail, asking what was going on over on Kauai and "What land, or lands, Henry Aki plans on having petitions filed?" The new airmail service brought a prompt reply. "Please be informed," wrote Hurley, "that he refers to the lease to the Kekaha Sugar Company...he said that he 'will see that the Hawaiians get a chance to own their own homes.'"

Now even the Hawaiians were after the Kekaha lands. Aki wrote Princess Kawananakoa, a member of the Hawaiian Homes Commission, regarding lands for the Hawaiians on the Mana and Kekaha uplands. These were Hawaiian Homes Lands, and Hawaiian homesteaders, by law, should receive first choice.

Territorial Land Commissioner Whitehouse expressed no concern for the Hawaiians or their rights to the land. In an amazingly unconciliatory letter to the Hawaiian Princess, he said that "since I have not received any notice from the Hawaiian Homes Commission that it is the intention of the Commission to select portions of the above mentioned lands for their use...it is the intention of this office to lease again these lands."

San Francisco's Rodiek wrote again in December renewing his lease proposal for the entire acreage, further proposing "that

the cost of purchasing the present mill or the erection of a new plant, should be deducted from the lease rental...by doing this, the Territory of Hawaii would own the entire project with all operating factors at expiration of the lease." Whitehouse could, with ease, have expressed interest in this proposal, of obvious benefit to the Territory. His reply was simply, "law does not permit this."

In the morning mail of May 10, 1938, Governor Poindexter received a bulky envelope from Kauai. It contained a petition of twenty-five names, requesting "twenty acre homesteading lots for cultivation of sugar cane or other products" on Kekaha sugar and grazing lands.

FOUR HUNDRED residents of Kauai were said to be ready to file, mostly farmers already skilled in sugar growing. They wanted their own farms and wished to move home and families onto the land, declaring this would not stop sugar production at Kekaha, but would result in independent farmers growing cane, which would be sold to the Kekaha Sugar mill for processing. The great water resources high in the Koke'e mountains, owned entirely by the government, would make it an easy matter not only to grow sugar cane, but to permit the development of private diversified farming and a dairy industry as well. Kekaha Sugar had already proved the feasibility of the homesteaders' arguments by operating their own truck farm on the very same Hawaiian Homes land.

In the end, the threat from the homesteaders was met easily by the industry. The planters had simply to point to a provision they had written into the homesteading law, a provision that excluded, from those Territory-owned lands available for homesteading, the lands leased to the sugar industry. Governor Poindexter, a Democratic appointee of President Franklin D. Roosevelt, stopped the homesteaders' plea for land by rejecting their petition. He backed up Whitehouse and members of the Board completely.

On June 8, 1938 the Kekaha lands were leased at public auction for the upset price of $130,000 to Kekaha Sugar Company. There were no other bidders.

World War II put a temporary end to the land debate. Kekaha was in full production, supplying sugar for the war effort. By 1942 Faye's upland plantation farms were producing more than 600,000 pounds of vegetables a year; clearly the land was suitable for truck farming, and Hawaiian farmers would have done well there. After supplying local markets, Kekaha sold surplus fresh produce to Kauai wholesalers in Lihu'e. Large quantities were also consumed by the Army and some even found their way to Honolulu. By 1943, 800,000 pounds of produce were being harvested, principally beans, corn, summer squash, cabbage, potatoes, tomatoes, carrots, rutabaga, lettuce, peas—almost anything that Faye could find seeds to plant.

At the end of World War II, Hal Hanna, Territorial Representative from Maui, reopened the land debate. Speaking before the Legislature, he stated, "Former Territorial Land Commissions literally gave thousands of acres of Hawaii's land leases to the big interests of the Territory for a mere song." He claimed that the Territory realized only $139,000 yearly for pasture lands and

The hanging valley of Awa'awapuhi if inaccessible except by footpaths and rock scrambles from adjacent Nu'alolo-'aina.

$290,000 yearly for sugar and pineapple lands, at the rate of only seven or eight dollars a year per acre. "Total revenue to the Territory from all land leases per year is only $1,247,891." Considering the large amount of government land under lease, Hanna concluded that "in a community as wealthy as Hawaii, somebody is getting away with something. The Territory receives too little."

The legislative flurry died quickly. While appointed Governor Ingram Stainback echoed Hanna's charges, Republicans representing sugar interests still controlled the majority vote and quietly pigeonholed in committee the bills introduced by Hanna. Not until statehood, fifteen years later, was any serious attempt made to revise Hawaii's public-land laws.

DURING THE LAST DAYS of the first political campaigns for state offices, Republican-appointed Governor William F. Quinn responded to the growing dissatisfaction of Hawaii's land-hungry residents and revived the plea Kauai's citizens had made two decades before. Quinn proposed a "second Mahele" and in a program designed to have wide popular appeal he suggested opening up large areas of public land on all the islands for sale. Included in his proposal were all of Kekaha Sugar Company's mauka cane and pasture lands. Undoubtedly guessing that the plan was nothing more than a political gambit and that the proposal would never be implemented, Kekaha refused to take the gubernatorial candidate seriously.

Hawaii was treated to the unusual spectacle of its Democrats opposing a land-reform program. They considered the Republican Mahele a great hoax, arguing that the bulk of the lands to be sold were already under long-term lease for sugar and cattle. They claimed that selling this land to individuals would "wreck the sugar industry" and "destroy the agricultural industry."

Quinn won the election, but failed to gain the backing of Kauai Senator Francis Ching, a Republican and the chairman of the Lands Committee, for legislation to put into effect a second Mahele.

Kekaha expanded its land-reclamation program even as the Legislature prepared to overhaul the public-land laws. An extensive drainage canal and pumping system was installed, capable of handling 80 million gallons a day for irrigation and pumping another 40 million gallons of swamp seepage into the sea. Sandy flatlands and drained lowlands were filled with bagasse, sugar-mill trash, and mud from cane washing equipment, then flooded with waste water to speed up decomposition in an organic land-recovery program. The new land was planted in cane or used for irrigated pasture and alfalfa. Intensive land use continued to be a major program at Kekaha in its efforts to increase land production to its maximum.

In the winter of 1953 Kekaha Sugar signed a new lease with the Territory of Hawaii for an upset annual rental of $201,608 for 28,021 acres. As usual, there were no other bidders for the lease, which would not expire until December 1968.

Fortune magazine once spoke of the system that keeps Hawaiian agriculture from collapsing in a competitive world as "paternalistic semi-feudalism." The system depends on control by a single industry over private and public lands. With state-

hood the system and the land laws that perpetuated it became obsolete. By common agreement among legislators, the 1961 regular session of the Legislature was to be a "land Legislature." It was to be, but it failed to pass a new land law, despite numerous extensions granted by the Governor for further meetings of the Senate-House Conference Committee, which was attempting to hammer out a compromise land law.

THE NEXT LEGISLATURE, a year later, successfully compromised by agreeing that the final determination of land exchanges and sale of public lands for public use would be by legislative act. But the main body of Hawaii's land laws went unchanged and the political struggle over land reform would continue to be a major issue in future elections.

Kauai carpenter Leonard Pope, hoping to become a truck farmer, showed up with friends at the state land auction on May 4, 1978, prepared to outbid McBryde Sugar Company for eleven acres of river bottom caneland in Hanapepe valley. They had gathered with crisp hundred dollar bills, getting whispered advice from bystanders. It was to be a spirited auction of state-owned lands. History repeating itself — David and Goliath on the sugar fields of Hawaii.

McBryde Sugar manager Philip Conrad solemnly opened bidding at the $475 a year upset price for the parcel. Carpenter Pope, facing Conrad in the small standing group, took him on, raising the ante to $500. He could easily pay for that with eleven acres of rotating vegetable crops. Conrad wanted the caneland and returned with a $600 bid. Pope raised it $50 and Conrad followed with a $100 call. Competitive bidding for caneland was a rare event on Kauai and the small crowd smiled cautiously as bidding continued to be passed back and forth in small increments, until McBryde Sugar finally prevailed with a high bid of $2,200. Farmer-to-be Pope and partner Sherwood Conant were disappointed but accepted their defeat nonchalantly in an auction they had little hope of winning. "I think there's some potential there," said Pope. "The only problem is, we didn't win it."

The Kekaha Sugar Company lease with the Territory of Hawaii expired in 1968. The new landlord was now a state, but the procedure was the same. The acreage was slightly lower from their last lease, 27,833 acres, and the upset price had doubled in fifteen years to $413,800. But the 11:00 a.m. auction procedure on the steps of the state office building in downtown Lihue on December 30, 1968, was quite familiar. Kekaha bid the upset price and the auctioneer's hammer went down with no higher bidder heard from. Bottomley and Sutton were not present to raise the bid five dollars for the sake of appearances. Kekaha was in the sugar business again for another fifteen years.

The voice of sugar became dominant not only in Hawaii's economy and politics but also in a plea for conservation of the land. In later years, as tourism gradually replaced sugar, pineapple and ranching as the industry leader in the island economy, the corporate land monopoly, on which the plantation system was based, helped preserve open space and valuable scenic resources that otherwise would have been subdivided and sold off by smaller owners, to be irretrievably lost. Land monopoly in Hawaii became a positive environmental asset.□

The bog of Alaka'i protects an indigenous forest of considerable vitality, yet still subject to destruction by the intrusion of alien biotica.

NOW, LET US annex the islands. Think how we could build up that whaling trade! Let us annex. We could make sugar enough there to supply all America, perhaps, and the prices would be very easy with the duties removed. And then we would have such a fine half-way house for our Pacific-plying ships; and such a convenient supply depot and such a commanding sentry-box for an armed squadron; and we could raise cotton and coffee there and make it pay pretty well, with the duties off and capital easier to get at. And then we would own the mightiest volcano on earth—Kilauea! Barnum could run it—he understands fires now. Let us annex, by all means. We could pacify Prince Bill and other nobles easily enough—put them on a reservation. Nothing pleases a savage like a reservation—a reservation where he has his annual hoes, and Bibles and blankets to trade for powder and whisky—a sweet Arcadian retreat fenced in with soldiers. By annexing, we would get all those 50,000 natives cheap as dirt, with their morals and other diseases thrown in. No expense for education—they are already educated; no need to convert them—they are already converted; no expense to clothe them—or obvious reasons.

We *must* annex those people. We can afflict them with our wise and beneficent governments. We can introduce the novelty of thieves, all the way up from street-car pickpockets to municipal robbers and Government defaulters, and show them how amusing it is to arrest them and try them and then turn them loose—some for cash and some for "political influence." We can make them ashamed of their simple and primitive justice…We can give them juries composed entirely of the most simple and charming leatherheads. We can give them railway corporations who will buy their Legislature like old clothes, and run over their best citizens and complain of the corpses for smearing their unpleasant juices on the track. We can let them have Connolly; we can loan them Sweeny; we can furnish them some Jay Goulds who will do away with their old-time notion that stealing is not respectable. We can confer Woodhull and Claflin on them. And George Francis Train. We can give them lecturers! I will go myself.

We can make that little bunch of sleepy islands the hottest corner on earth, and array it in the moral splendor of our high and holy civilization. Annexation is what the poor islanders need. "Shall we to men benighted, the lamp of life deny?"

— Mark Twain
Hartford, Jan. 6, 1873.

Waipo'o stream is intercepted by a Kekaha sugar company irrigation ditch diverting water from Alaka'i swamp. Waipo'o falls exist only when the ditch overflows.

The great panorama of Kauai island is seen in the rocky gulch of arid Waimea canyon and the cold leaves of tropical plants in wet Alaka'i swamp. Together they embrace a geological masterpiece of nature that is beautiful right to the edges. Even the blemishes appear to be the right kind.

The Native Forest Begins to Disappear

The Hawaiian forest, long avoided by Hawaiians, who feared its strange inhabitants, and by white men, who had no immediate use for it, finally began to recede, and as the forest went, the quality and dependability of water went too. The industry saw the threat, and acted.

PERHAPS AS RECENTLY as the time of Christ, Kauai was covered with a great native forest. Giant *koa* and ohi'a lehua cast shade for ie'ie and fragile ferns. Hawaiian loulu palms grew in dense thickets, vying for their places in the sun on gently rising slopes. The ground cover was tropical, rich, and various.

How long ago this forest flourished, and when it died, is open to conjecture, but no human came in time to see it. When the first Polynesians arrived from Tahiti in their long, double-hulled canoes, tall reeds had flaunted their brown tassels for centuries in the Koloa swamp, where the forest once stood. Breezes blowing off the nearby Hoary Head mountains rippled the dark waters where duck, heron, and mudhen lived undisturbed, swimming over or wading among the logs of the old forest, which were to be discovered by white men centuries later.

The forest had retreated to higher ground and stood undisturbed and unknown, except perhaps by the Menehune, Mu, and Akua. The Menehune, according to Hawaiian legend, were tiny forest people, very industrious, who worked only at night and abandoned any project that was not completed by dawn. They had defeated and driven off most of the Mu people, their neighbors, in ancient times long before the first Polynesians. Hawaiians did not fear the Menehune, who were good natured and whose supernatural power was limited, but they feared the Akua, who were giant, malevolent, and whose cruel and deformed visages were reproduced on Hawaiian masks. Fear of the Akua kept Hawaiians out of their country. Fear of them, and of other things in the forest: stones inexplicably warm in the night, whisperings, sudden violent rainstorms, spirits walking tall and white in the treetops.

Few Hawaiians ventured into the deep forests—only the bird collectors, gathering feathers for the great capes of the Ali'i, and woodsmen searching for koa canoe logs. These men moved through the forest without appreciably altering it. The woodsmen took few trees and they left little trace of their presence. Neither did the bird collectors, called kiamanu, though they made their home in the forests for long periods in their efforts to supply the bright red, yellow, green, and black feathers demanded by flamboyant kings. Once the needed feathers were plucked, most birds were set free.

The native Hawaiians confined their trails generally to ridge tops, from fear of the deep forest below, and there they had little effect on the woods. The only Hawaiian tools for cutting canoe logs were stone blades and fire, and the difficulty of the work prevented cutting more trees than necessary.

Hawaiians began to see more of the wooded mountains late in the eighteenth century, when the chiefs learned from white traders of the wealth to be had from selling sandalwood to China. The fragrant wood had been discovered in 1791 on Kauai by Captain Kendrick. By 1886, when sandalwood logging ceased, the fragrant tree was almost exterminated.

Kamehameha the First's successful military campaigns to conquer all the Hawaiian Islands were undoubtedly financed substantially by the sale of sandalwood in Canton, which enriched the King and chiefs of Hawaii by an estimated three to four million dollars in money and goods. Little of this wealth filtered down to the common people, who sometimes were away in the mountains for several weeks cutting the valuable wood. It sold for from $8.00 to $10.00 a picul (a weight of about 133 pounds), the amount one man could supposedly carry on his back from the forest.

The King's sudden wealth made him easy prey for eager traders, and large drafts on the King's meager cash account compelled him to demand even greater labor from the natives, who were forced to work months in the forest without compensation. When sandalwood became scarce, the King placed a *kapu* on the wood, reserving it for himself. Large trees that a man could not reach around could not be cut, and the trampling of seedlings was punished by a fine.

THE OPPRESSION of the chiefs in their drive for personal wealth and service to the King became tyrannical as it became more difficult to find and harvest marketable logs. The people suffered cruelly, many dying of exposure in the wet mountains. Neglect of taro patches and crops almost precipitated a famine. An annual tax of one picul of sandalwood was levied upon the commoner, who was forced under penalty of fine to bring out even the remaining small crooked sticks, which were fit only for incense in Chinese joss houses. Almost all the larger and more accessible trees had been cut when the sandalwood trade finally ended, and the King was actually in debt, despite the wealth harvested from the Hawaiian forests.

Except for the sandalwood destruction, the white man's coming did not at first greatly change the rain forest. For a time, there was even less forest use. The grotesque temple idols carved from tough ohi'a were now a forbidden pagan symbol. Spears were no longer needed. The largest, longest, and most magnificent specimens of koa had flourished in the valleys and narrow gulches where they grew high to reach the sun. These had been

A fragment of Waimea stream is revealed within the shadows of Waimea canyon before the early morning sun reaches the inner gorge.

cut for outrigger canoes and dragged from the forest by ancient routes. But now redwood logs were drifting ashore onto Maha'ulepu beach. The chiefs' craftsmen chipped out the California logs into the largest war canoes in Hawaiian waters and soon found the much smaller native koa quite unsatisfactory.

The advent of the sugar industry and the introduction of a money economy also helped to protect the forest. Hawaiians bought cotton instead of making kapa from the stripped and pounded bark of the mamaki and hau trees. Rather than hike into the plentiful forests of ohi'a and hew timber posts and rafters for their grass huts, collecting armloads of pili grass for thatching and hardwood for poi boards and calabashes, they traded plantation credit coupons at the company store for lumber from Oregon.

Damage to the forest by native Hawaiians had been negligible however, and any accidental protection the white man gave the forest during his early days in Hawaii was offset by what he did later. After the arrival of cattle and goats on Captain Vancouver's vessels, in 1793, the destruction of Hawaii's forests was inevitable. It was accelerated by the fateful combination of royal *kapu* on hunting the animals and the absence of hard winters to check their reproduction. There were no predators and there was a limitless food supply. Increasing numbers of pigs added to the forest devastation, and foothills and mountain slopes throughout the kingdom were quickly denuded by feral animals moving higher and higher up the green hillsides. Enormous areas became wastelands as a result of uncontrolled depredation from summit peaks to the sea.

As the Hawaiian people slowly died from venereal diseases, measles, smallpox, influenza, and other Old World curses brought in by traders and sailors, so the virgin forest was killed, in many areas to the last tree. Construction of a road or even a trail was invariably followed by death of native trees and ground cover. Few, if any, residents at that time had knowledge of the tropical rain forest and its quick dieback when it is imposed upon, even to the slightest degree. Only a thin layer of humus soil covered the fanlike reach of the ohi'a lehua root system. The very shallow roots were shaded by delicate ferns and shrubs of the rain-forest ground cover. The luxuriant ie'ie vines hanging from forest trees, the *ti* and banana plants, and many of the ferns and native sedges could not survive Vancouver's cattle.

BY 1815, THE WILD CATTLE were recognized as a menace to the forest and their hunting was no longer forbidden, but they continued to multiply rapidly. Early ranchers on Kauai began to graze the wild cattle commercially as the growing population demanded meat. The native forest was pushed back by the cattle to the edges of Alaka'i Swamp and the steep pali of Wai'ale'ale, and the forest shrank to a tenth of its original size.

Sound range-management practices were unknown or ignored by ranchers, who pushed their cattle continuously onward into the forest as feed was consumed, many times deliberately setting fire to the trees and ground cover to open the way for new feed grasses. Steep pali, shunned altogether by cattle, were laid bare by goats. Wild pigs tore up tree ferns to eat the starchy core and rooted destructively in the rich soil.

Grazing lands no longer existed in the lowlands. Where sugar was not growing, earlier farmers had already stripped the land and erosion was far advanced. Huge red scars of exposed earth snaked up the steep ridges, and frequent rain squalls began to soil the blue ocean red where silted throats of mountain streams emptied into the sea. Whaling men in their turn abused the Hawaiian forests. The warm waters of the Pacific and the trade winds of Hawaii made the islands a haven from 1819 to 1871 for the hundreds of Yankee ships searching for whale oil. At times thirty ships waited offshore from tiny Koloa landing. In 1853, 535 whaling vessels visited the Hawaiian Islands, and Koloa on Kauai along with Lahaina, on Maui, became a favored port for semiannual refitting, repairing, and provisioning. Oil and bone were transferred to homeward-bound merchant ships.

OLONA FIBER, which grew deep inside the wet forest, became prized by the sailors for harpoon lines. Native timbers were used for minor ship repairs, and kukui forests in the Hoary Head range of Koloa was stripped to provide fuel for rendering pots.

Discovery of gold in California midway in the nineteenth century spurred the sugar industry to expand rapidly to supply the new western market, which was much closer to Hawaii than to southern and Caribbean growers. The early planters were not concerned with preserving the integrity of the native forests, and thousands of acres of virgin jungle were burned to prepare the land for cultivation. Beyond the cane fields, work crews felled trees to supply fuel for the steam-engine boilers of the grinding mills. Then more firewood was cut to boil the raw sugar juice. Some plantations, with an unbelievable lack of foresight, cut into the watersheds that fed their expensive ditch systems.

It was only with the advent of coal and oil-fired boilers, supplemented by dry cane waste, that cutting native timber for fuel began to cease.

Severe insect damage accompanied grazing damage, and portions of native forests were badly hurt by insects which gained a foothold on nearby denuded areas. Insects almost completely defoliated ohia lehua growing in high, wet valleys. Koa was periodically defoliated by upwards of a dozen insect enemies, which at times have threatened its extinction. The sugar industry's first collaborative program with government agencies began with broad programs to eradicate insects by introducing parasites.

Great forest fires swept woodlands with appalling regularity. Hawaiians started fires to clear small parcels, and trade winds would sweep the flames up pandanus-covered slopes. Probably the most destructive fire in all Hawaii swept the plateau above Mana on Kauai toward the end of the nineteenth century. Valdemar Knudsen, returning in an open boat from the nearby island of Niihau, saw a rising cloud of smoke and quickly made for Kauai, but by the time he and his men arrived in the uplands, the entire forest was aflame. It was impossible to stop the fire, and it burned for weeks, scorching the ridge of distant Miloli'i Valley on Napali, before a torrential rainstorm drowned the flames. More than 10,000 acres of native forest, already injured by wild cattle and ruinous overgrazing practices, was destroyed in the blaze.

Awa'awapuhi valley shelters a forest of native kukui trees and wild taro still growing in ruins of taro patches constructed centuries ago.

What the cattle overlooked and fire failed to engulf, planters and ranchers removed in a consuming desire to get rich on the newly available lands of Hawaii, which were obtainable for little investment beyond the cost of land clearing.

SMALL SUGAR GROWERS proliferated rapidly and as quickly failed; their lack of agricultural knowledge and insufficient operating capital doomed their enterprises, leaving the cleared forest lands temporarily abandoned to rank weeds and rapidly eroding gullies. Others planted coffee, mulberry, cotton, and various commercial crops that also failed. There was such an abundance of land that few businessmen questioned the feasibility of their projected planting. If they had, thousands of acres of fertile land would have been saved. A planters' Gold Rush swept the Islands, to be eventually stopped by concerted efforts of the very sugar monopoly repeatedly criticized for selfish exploitation of Hawaii's land.

The destruction of the forest began to concern the sugar planters, who were among the first to realize that remedial action was needed. They moved quickly to restore the forests that had held water for the irrigation of their vast sugar fields, before increasing soil erosion and polluted water sources endangered the recharging ability of underground water tables. In 1876, by request of the sugar growers, the King proclaimed a law for "the protection and preservation of woods and forests" and actually set aside an area of the upper lands of Hamakua and Kohala on the Island of Hawaii as a forest preserve—but little was done to enforce the early law.

Shortly before the Kingdom was overthrown by annexationists, Queen Lili'uokalani signed into law legislation that exempted from taxes private lands exclusively used to protect watersheds. Approved in 1892, the unique law stated that "The preservation of forests is a matter of great public interest in consequence of their influence upon the water supply of the Kingdom," and provided that "where land is fenced to protect the forest, springs or streams, and all livestock is excluded and no other use is made of the land, the owner will be exempt from taxes."

Actual forest reserves were not established by the Queen, and the large sugar plantation owners became more and more frightened by the continued destruction of the forest lands by unrestrained ranching operations.

Sanford Dole, in one of his first acts as new President of the Provisional Government of Hawaii, created a Bureau of Forestry and Agriculture in 1892, and reforestation work began on the bare, denuded hills back of Honolulu and the slopes of Punchbowl Crater. Work on Kauai was soon underway.

With communication with Washington a difficult procedure and political forces of the deposed Queen still at work, a Constitutional Convention met in May 1894 and drafted a constitution for a Republic, which was proclaimed on July 4th, with Dole as its first president. The new Republic had many problems to meet and had little opportunity to develop a sound program for reforestation, although government and businessmen both realized the need and importance of a fully implemented forestry program. Many years were still to pass before the first forest reserve was actually established.

Hawaii was warned again in an 1895 report from the Minister of the Interior Herberts, who expressed his concern that:

The destruction of forests in this country is a serious matter. Large areas of land have within recent years become deforested, and the effect on the climate in those regions is shown by the decreased rainfall. Ninety-nine percent of this destruction has and is being caused by cattle. It is most unfortunate that so large an amount of the public domain has been leased for grazing purposes, nearly all the forest lands are now under lease to cattle raisers, and unless something is soon done to preserve the limited amount of remaining forests they will, in a short time, be all destroyed.

Four years later, the Bureau of Forestry and Agriculture presented to the Republic the first detailed report on forest islands in 1899. In describing Kauai's Kalaheo forests Herberts said: Hundreds of acres of this forest land have been destroyed by cattle; hundreds of trees are dead and dying, and only a small portion of the forest close to the mountain ridge remains intact. Ninety per cent of the cattle I saw are in an advanced stage of tuberculosis—and some of the animals were mere walking skeletons too weak to brush off the horn flies. None of the cattle were fit for human food. On the lowlands near the sea, the cattle were in fair condition. If the McBryde Sugar Company do not take steps to fence off this forest land at once and (provide for) removal of worthless cattle, our government should take advantage of our forest laws and cancel the lease.

Island ranchers strongly objected when the sugar planters offered to construct, at their own expense, miles of fences to close off the remaining forests to grazing. The ranchers claimed that the fences would cut off their cattle from feed and water during dry periods in the lowlands, though they admitted that if grazing continued in the forest, it would simply be a question of time before the remaining forest was destroyed and the existing water sources disappeared permanently.

EARLY IN THE TWENTIETH century, Harold Lyons was employed by the sugar industry to bring order to land management before the sugar industry was ruined. He imported a handful of mainland foresters to plan a reforestation program and to investigate the nature of Hawaiian forests. The Hawaiian Sugar Planters Association took the lead in 1902, when they organized a special committee to consult with Sanford Dole, then first Governor of the Territory of Hawaii. Dole accepted their proposals and appointed men named by the sugar industry to designate forest reservation boundaries on private and public lands. The 1903 legislature, following the governor's recommendations, passed the first Territorial law providing for the establishment of forest reservations.

With the objective of devising ways and means to halt the forest destruction, and to determine forest reserve boundaries, government-appointed foresters, recruited and paid by the Sugar Planters Association, visited the ravaged forests and called meetings of planters and ranchers.

The voice of sugar became dominant not only in Hawaii's economy and politics, but also in a plea for conservation of the land.□

Freshwater streams flow cold and pure from fractures in internal volcanic dike systems, where light green Kukui leaves accentuate the topography of Kalalau.

OUT THERE WAS one tree specially dedicated to Kauai, and it made both life and agriculture on the island possible. Wherever the powerful northeast trades whipped sea and salt air inland, killing everything that grew, men had planted the strange, silky, gray-green casuarina tree, known sometimes as the ironwood. Groves of this curious tree, covered with ten-inch needles and seed cones that resembled round buttons, stood along the shore and protected the island. The foliage of the casuarina was not copious and to the stranger each tree looked so frail that it seemed about to die, but it possessed incredible powers of recuperation, and what it thrived on most was a harsh, salty trade wind that whipped its fragile needles into a frenzy and tore at its cherrybark trunk; for then the casuarina dug in and saved the island. The sea winds howled through its branches; its frail needles caught the salt; the force of the storm was broken and all who lived in the shadow of the casuarina tree lived securely.

— JAMES MICHENER, *Hawaii*

undoubtedly saved the sugar industry from ruin. The experiments with eucalyptus, paperbark, monkeypod, ironwood, black wattle, Monterey cypress, and silk oak were successful beyond all expectations.

Probably the first trees planted in the Kauai mountains were planted by Ranger Albert MacDonald in 1928. They were 100 seedlings of Kauai's indigenous koa acacia, kaua'iensis, and the 324 acacia koa around the Kanalohuluhulu meadow in Koke'e. In the same year, Albert Duval traveled by horseback to the edge of Alaka'i Swamp along Wai'alae Stream and planted ten California redwood and fifteen firebush seedlings.

Numerous varieties of trees continued to be introduced throughout the islands without any over-all plan. In 1929, the Army Air Corps, as a community service, helped the foresters sow seed in denuded areas of Pu'ukapele, Koke'e, and Napali. From a Fokker C-2 monoplane, fifty-eight pounds of New Zealand karaka seed, which turned out to be poisonous, were scattered on higher slopes of Alaka'i from 2,000 feet above the swamp. A total of 1,689 pounds of seed was sown from the air at random over a widespread area. Most of these were Pride of India seeds, but included were Chinese fan palm, ironwood, Java plum, eucalyptus robusta, and African tulip. Also sown were seeds of two natives, kukui and loulu palm.

The game warden at Koke'e planted Oregon ash, dogwood, elderberry and huckleberry, and liberated twenty-four young guinea fowl. The mongrel forest of Koke'e continued to grow.

Wild cattle, goats, and pigs, with no natural enemies, continued to threaten the planting program. Duval estimated that 20 per cent of new tree losses were to wild pig rooting, and 10 per cent from the uluhe fern, which smothered young seedlings.

On his first inspection trip to Kalalu Valley after the old Hawaiian Napali trail was cleared by the county in early 1933, Duval reported to Chief Forester Judd on the continued overgrazing by cattle, which had practically exterminated ferns and ti on the ridges. He wrote, "Cattle foraging on the steep slopes during wet weather have cut trails into the soft earth creating channels whereby soil is being washed into the ocean." On the same trip, he noted many wild goats, "as many as 40 in a single herd." Wild cattle and goats still roamed the forests in great numbers, contributing to continued erosion and to destruction of plants along Napali.

PROBABLY THE MOST destructive exotic plant introduction occurred about 1920, when a young plantation manager, Dave Larsen, carried to Koke'e several cuttings of Himalayan blackberries, planting them in the backyard of his mountain cabin on Noe stream. Neighbor Charlie Rice apprehensively watched the blackberry spread into the forest, and he notified Territorial Forester Judd of the potential danger to Koke'e. Although the cabin owners pulled the brambles from their own yards, the territory neglected to take similar measures on forest lands. It was not until several years later that Territorial Ranger MacDonald saw blackberry sprouts growing along the Waineke trail and began pulling up every shoot in sight. He traced the berry to Larsen's then-abandoned cabin, and with the help of a CCC crew, swiftly dug up the original blackberry patch, now grown into a wild tangle of thorns. They cut out the roots and

sifted the soil. But within a year, new sprouts appeared in the woods. The blackberries had escaped. Birds soon spread them throughout Koke'e, where their vines gradually smothered the life from ferns and ground cover.

During World War II, all forestry programs stopped. The Army took over the mountains of Kauai, and during four war years the blackberry grew unrestricted. MacDonald returned after the war and was shocked at what he found. "I was sick when I saw the blackberries everywhere," he said. "They were too far gone to stop them."

OTHER FOREIGN EXOTICS had escaped and spread through the tropical forest. The bright nasturtiums were first planted by Ebba Faye in the yard of her mountain house at Halemanu. Early construction workers planted the hanging pink lilikoi around their bunk dormitories for food while digging the Kekaha irrigation tunnels in 1923. Calla lilies were first seen about the same time. Montbretia, the small bright red lily, was well-established by 1905. The purple flowered "Isenberg bush" was brought to Kauai from the foothills of the Himalayas by Dora Isenberg and carefully tended in her garden. The attractive tibouchina plant soon escaped from her Lihu'e home and spread into the foothills of Kilohana crater. In about 1909 Mrs. Abner Wilcox brought from Honolulu a small multiblossomed lantana plant potted in a red bowl. She enjoyed the tiny orange and pink blossoms for many years until the plant grew too large for the porch. Her gardener threw it out on the trash pile, from where it eventually spread to all parts of the island. The bush grew into impenetrable thickets and thrived on the dry ridges and flats laid bare by goats and cattle. Guava, another exotic, grew into impenetrable thickets, gradually choking out competitive plant life. Java plum filled gulches from rim to rim and native plants completely disappeared.

The tropical forest beauty was slowly and irretrievably being replaced by a synthetic forest. Human experiments were changing the shape and color of the land. Broad carpets of a giant grass, sugar cane, covered the flatlands between gulches. Many streams never reached the sea in summer months, their full flow intercepted by complex irrigation systems and carried to the thirsty cane fields which consumed many times more water than a city covering the same area would have.

Gray patterns of pineapples covered plateaus in geometric forms, and contour planting began to reshape the land on upper hillsides. Kauai, as first sighted by the Polynesians, was barely recognizable. Efforts to stimulate economic development had succeeded beyond all measure. The government encouraged importation of European labor. Workers came in large numbers from Portugal, Germany, England, Scotland, and Norway. Contract workers left their homes in China, Japan and the Philipines for promises of new wealth in Hawaii. Grants of land to foreigners to encourage permanent settlers changed the tiny Island Kingdom's subsistence economy to a modern money economy, and into a territory of the United States.

But Hawaii had become poorer by another measure. Its native forests were virtually destroyed and would never recover. In less than 150 years, man had destroyed a forest and an eco-system that was 20 to 30 million years in the making. □

Introduced pink poha smothers indigenous acasia koa in Koke'e.

The Mountain Becomes a Forest Park

The old foresters had made Pandora's mistake; they were followed by public servants who knew better, and the forest had a new chance.

FROM THE TIME Valdemar Knudsen first turned his herd into the uplands of Kokee, ranchers had grazed cattle in the high forests there. Later sugar planters came and marveled at the wonders of Kokee as they supervised the digging of the extensive irrigation ditches and tunnels which were to divert water from mountain streams along the upper rim of Waimea Canyon. They were among the first to enjoy a wilderness experience in the natural beauty of Kokee. These transient visitors slowly became aware of their responsibility toward the forest and the need for its care and preservation.

Conservation became the law of the land. Conservation to save the sugar industry, however, not conservation for recreation or timber production. Multiple use of any sort was still frowned upon as potentially harmful to the watershed.

Kauai's forest lands were ringed with cattle-proof fences and padlocked. Even public picnicking and camping were discouraged. Hunting continued by cowboys and plantation workers, but primarily as a means to supplement their food. Effective game management did not exist. Tourism had not been thought of, nor was it ever considered by kama'aina landowners that any economic activity could replace sugar.

But recreation began in the forests of Koke'e, in spite of the fences. The wagon trail along the rim of Waimea Canyon was gradually improved and soon Kauai's first automobiles clashed gears on the steep grades out of Kekaha. Knudsen's friends discovered the cool, invigorating air of Kokee and built small cabins of their own in the forest. Lumber was hauled up the winding road, and an exclusive mountain community quickly developed on Knudsen-leased land at Halemanu.

Governor Charles J. McCarthy made his first visit to the Kokee mountains on vacation after World War I. He agreed that more land should be opened up for cabins, and 415 acres were withdrawn from the Kekaha ranch lease. By proclamation of the Governor, the land was transferred to the County of Kauai, which leased the cabin sites. Surveys of the land were vague, and in the surveyors language spirit of the time, the boundary corner monument along Waimea Canyon rim was described in the proclamation as "a mound of stones around trunk of leaning koa tree." It is no wonder that the exact location of the first county park on Kauai was not determined for many years.

The Governor of Hawaii, following a visit to Koke'e in 1929, expressed a desire to increase the area of protected forest reserve and to include the road area along the rim of Waimea Canyon, "the idea being to preserve the koa trees along this road for the scenic effect."

Forester Judd personally inspected the area on the ground on a three-day survey trip and came to the conclusion that an area of almost 9,000 acres could be added to the Pu'u Ka Pele Forest Reserve without impairing ranching operations, which were marginal at best. Most of the land, especially along the seacoast,

was relatively inaccessible country, much of it covered with scrub forest growth and just beginning to recover from the damaging 1890 range fire.

Some meadows and pockets of good grazing existed among the recovering groves of koa trees at the head of small gulches along Waimea Canyon, and it was from these sections that Forester Judd especially wanted all stock excluded "so as to give the young tree growth a chance to mature." In his report, Judd pointed out that "the constant nibbling by cattle and horses of young koa seedlings and root sprouts and the smashing of young koa trees by cattle...simply holds back the growth development of the trees. So long as grazing is permitted...proper tree growth and a satisfactory undercover of shrubs and other vegetation will not be obtained...The practice of allowing grazing on areas where it is desired to have and maintain native forest growth has become archaic."

However, the continuing requirements of the ranchers, who grazed their cattle with little restraint and without proper range management practices, were not to be ignored. C. T. Bailey, Commissioner of Public Lands, was obviously not convinced of the necessity of expanding forest reserves in 1929 to accelerate recovery of the native forest. He informed Forester Judd that his proposal "seems inadvisable on account of the grazing value of this land...with the resultant loss of rental to the Territory and the economic loss in curtailing the production of cattle." Instead of Judd's 9,000 acres, Bailey recommended the forest expansion be limited to approximately 750 acres, almost all along the Waimea Canyon Rim Road. The compromise left more than 8,000 acres of slowly recovering forest land exposed to continued depredation by cattle.

IN AUGUST 1930, 755 acres were added to the Pu'u Ka Pele Forest Reserve, including the small groves of koa and ohi'a, and growths of new sandalwood and native hibiscus. Within a few years, these 755 acres, insufficient as they might be, were proclaimed the Waimea Canyon Territorial Park.

In 1941, Joseph F. Kunesh, director of the short-lived Territorial Planning Board, stated that:

Although the Territory owns over one and a half million acres in 9,600 parcels well distributed on all the islands and controls over a million acres of public and private forest reserve lands, there are in Hawaii today practically no Territorial parks, no Territorial parkways, no Territorial monuments, or no Territorial memorials.

Ten years later, following the end of World War II, the words were almost as true as when first written. The planters' policy of closed forest reserves not only had prevented the establishment of a timber industry, but also had stopped the formation of a modern Territorial park system.

'Ohi'a lehua on the rim of Kalalau valley.

The National Park Service observed in a report for the Territory that "It is doubtful if a completely successful park and recreation program can be achieved in the Territory without a higher degree of participation by private citizens, organizations, and most especially the large land holders, than seems to have been provided heretofore…a favorable 'climate' is the first prerequisite for programs of this order."

Growing public clamor for mountain parks soon made itself heard, however, and the Territorial government, while still sympathetic to the contrary wishes of the sugar industry, could hardly ignore the growing Hawaiian middle class who desired outdoor recreation and pointed out the famed California system of state parks as an example for Hawaii to follow.

Hawaiian residents began traveling more widely on the mainland, and their favorable experiences in popular state parks strongly influenced local politicians. Territorial Representative Manuel Aguiar of Kauai early in 1947 asked the Board of Agriculture and Forestry, which had jurisdiction over Territorial lands, to make Koke'e and Napali a state park. Colin G. Lennox, president of the Board, prepared an administration bill to establish a Koke'e Territorial Park on forest reserve lands. Introduced in 1947, the bill never left committee in the Republican, planter-dominated legislature.

PUBLIC DISAPPOINTMENT over these events and growing awareness of the need for care and protection of the forest lands caused many community organizations to discuss alternate ways and means of opening up the mountain lands of Kauai for public use. Possibly the first citizen plea for a national park on Kauai resulted from this frustrated political agitation for a Territorial park in Koke'e. The Hanapepe Civic Association wrote Colin Lennox after the 1947 legislature adjourned without bringing about a Koke'e Park, saying, "Frankly, the National Park Service should have established several areas on the island of Kauai as national parks, especially that of the Koke'e and Napali coast." They added further that "This Association will back any effort that you make or endorse in regard to national parks on the island of Kauai." The seed for a national park was planted early by the people of Kauai.

Two years later, Act 185 of the 1949 legislature called for withdrawal of 4,451 acres from the Napali-Kona Forest Reserve and set aside the lands as a Territorial Park. Cheers by park supporters were muted somewhat by the discovery that no funds were appropriated for the infant park. Also, the boundaries were not selected on the basis of recreation or scenic potential, but rather to connect existing survey points in order to make a field survey unnecessary. Three years passed before Governor Oren E. Long on May 15, 1952, officially proclaimed the existence of the Koke'e Territorial Park and construction began on the first true public facilities: a natural history museum, to be staffed by volunteers; a grocery store; and four rental cabins, all constructed mostly from surplus army camp materials. Koke'e had finally become a public park.

A progressive island-born forester, Eric Reppun, was appointed new president of the Board of Agriculture and Forestry by the first part-Hawaiian governor, Samuel Wilder King, to take on the task of changing completely the philosophy of a department held tightly in the grip of the sugar planters for 40 years.

The forests had been locked up and unused—except as the large land owners wanted them available for expansion of pasture or cane. The forest reserve laws were written to allow assignment of privately owned land to forest reserves—where the land would be free from taxes—yet permitted withdrawal of the land at any time on ten days' notice. Not until 1957 were these liberal surrender agreements changed to halt the establishment of temporary forest reserves to avoid land taxes while the land was held for future use.

The planters and large landowners lost much of their control over the land with passage of new land laws in 1957. Reppun proceeded to eliminate industry influence over the Division of Forestry and to restore the prestige of the Territorial Forester and the Board of Agriculture and Forestry. The board members unwittingly had become titular figures in Honolulu who simply approved actions the island associate forester had often already performed. The old Board of Agriculture and Forestry seldom met and internal communication had suffered, with the result that the associate forester usually ran his own island and developed policies as he saw fit, without guidelines based on long-term best interests of the people of the Territory.

The island foresters were really only custodians—and too often only self-made naturalists. Their old habits were not easily broken. The established foresters were the same men who years before had been selected by the Hawaiian Sugar Planters Association, hired by the Territory and paid by the Planters Association. Their wages were now paid by the Territory, but their loyalties were to the planters, and the old timers somewhat resented the new personnel and the new programs. To them, the interests of the sugar industry were identical with the interests of the Territory. They resisted the new young men in Honolulu who wanted wider use of the forest—a complete departure from the planters' idea. Reppun was the first appointed forester not a part of the Establishment, and he was severely criticized by the planters' representatives for breaking with traditional patterns of forest management that had served industry so well since the days of the Hawaiian monarchy.

Reppun died before he was able to complete the long-needed overhaul of the forestry division. The Territorial Governor picked Wayne Collins to carry on Reppun's program. Collins, the last president of the soon to be reorganized Board of Agriculture and Forestry, resigned his position as a popular Honolulu television news director and prepared to implement the new concepts of forest use. For his deputy, Collins appointed Hawaii Island forester Bill Bryan, who traveled tirelessly to every island and convinced the old-timers of the new program's rightness. Islanders still speak of Bryan as the "old tough man" who, in six months, was able to get a commercial timber planting program under way for the "young tough man," as the independent and somewhat uncompromising Collins was called.

For the first time since the days of the CCC, improvements were made on recreation trails. Collins ordered the removal of miles of forest reserve fences, opening the reserves for public recreation and park use. He laid the groundwork for a new public appreciation of forest lands.

The government of Hawaii, through Collins, was responding to the wishes of a larger number of people as the fiftieth state savored its first taste of statehood. □

Fern Grotto State Park on the Wailua river is peaceful and quiet only between the swarms of tourists brought upstream by motorized barge. Its dripping water source depends on a leaky sugar irrigation reservoir in the cane fields above.

Trying to Build a Road All the Way

*The most beautiful valley of the Napali coast,
undisturbed until the twentieth century, was
threatened suddenly and in turn by cattle, lantana,
wild cats, and politicians.*

IN THE ANCIENT DAYS, Hawaiians living in the hanging valleys of Napali on the north coast of Kauai celebrated important events with a great feast and native fireworks. A favorite place for the rare events was remote Nualolo Kai, a shallow valley with a beach at its mouth and a half-moon reef arching out into the sea. At the evening's climax when all had finished their feasting and drunk their brew of 'okolehao, young children climbed to the top of the high vertical cliffs guarding Nualolo. Here were piles of *hau* and hollow *papala* branches, gathered earlier from the mountains and cut into lengths of ten and twenty feet. Fires were lighted and as the dry, light sticks blazed, they were pushed from the pali into space, and the evening winds carried them far out to sea. Then darker night closed in, and the villagers and chiefs slept where they had gathered on the beach.

Hawaiian village fires were burning in adjacent Nualolo Aina Valley at least 700 years ago, as evidenced by carbon dates determined by Bishop Museum archeologists. Thriving communities flourished in the narrow valleys. The Napali taro plant, famous throughout the kingdom for its keeping qualities, was cultivated in the deep black earth. Stone-walled terraces and diversion ditches feeding water to the taro patches completely covered the valley floor. House platforms were built high on the talus slopes or wedged between terrace dikes so they would not infringe on the valuable taro land.

This traditional way of life continued into very recent times, but began to change as Hawaiians became more and more aware of the white man's offer of what might be a better life, and as the fertility of the land and the need for its produce changed with the times. Rancher Selwyn Robinson, who had become the largest individual landowner on Kauai, forsaw a voluntary Hawaiian emigration, and in return for deeds to their kuleana, provided the necessary cash for Hawaiians to buy Chinese rice, clothes from the merchants, white man's lumber, and to send their children to missionary schools. Robinson allowed the Hawaiians to continue to live on their kuleana and harvest the taro, but they soon yearned for the new amenities away from the valley and, by 1914, the valley of Kalalau and its rich taro lands were abandoned. Robinson claimed fee simple ownership or majority interest in 156 acres of unlocated kuleana—the only private land in Kalalau Valley.

Robinson obtained a long-term lease on the remaining government lands, and shipped in cattle to fatten on the rich grasses of Kalalau. As the grass was consumed, thickets of lantana and guava grew across the valley and into the abandoned taro terraces. The cattle denuded much of their grazing land, eating seedlings of native trees and every blade of sprouting grass. In places only the lantana and guava remained—apparently distasteful even to the hungry animals. The proliferating seeds spread out across the valley, sticking to the hides of foraging cattle or carried by tropic birds to the most remote ravines. Hoofs broke down the carefully constructed terraces and dikes, destroying native house platforms and heiau temples. Village sites disappeared in whirling dust fields, and once carefully tended taro terraces disappeared under silt and weeds.

Today the destruction continues. Kalalau is a virtual no man's land—neither forest reserve nor state park, rather a combination pot farm and campground with no one assuming responsibility for its care or maintenance. Hunters, arriving by boat and helicopter, roam the valley, mixing uneasily among family hiking groups and picnickers, shooting goats on the fluted cliffs, sometimes recovering the animals, more often than not leaving them to rot. Campers themselves show little inclination to clean up when their surroundings are so misused. Wild cats roam free, killing rare birds and robbing nests. The songs of Hawaiian birds—once filling the air with their haunting calls—have begun to disappear along with the native trees and endemic plants in which they built their nests. Grazing leases have since been cancelled and cattle removed, but crowds of nude campers clutter the beaches in souciant disregard of other visitors. Kalalau's only stream is used to clean goat eviscara and serves as a latrine for others. Only the sky and ocean remain clean.

ONLY KALALAU'S SIZE and its relative inaccessibility have kept it the most beautiful valley in the Pacific. So far the abuse has been on a scale that nature can handle. The four-thousand-foot cliffs, high waterfalls, and white beaches are still unsurpassed in all Hawaii. It is the visitors that are soiled.

In past years the greatest threat to Kalalau's beauty has been the bulldozer. Many local residents have long dreamed of a scenic highway around the island connecting the dead-end country roads at Koke'e and Ha'ena and crossing the spectacular cliffs of Napali the hanging valley of Hanakoa and Alaka'i Swamp. The obvious economic impracticality of a road through the mountains, and the ravage of the scenic Napali wilderness by a ruinous cut-and-fill highway, does not concern them. The road would divert into the heart of Kauai's greatest scenery all the obnoxious noise and smell of every truck, car, and motorcycle crossing the island, using Koke'e Park as a handy shortcut, and would result in destruction of the wilderness that the first major territorial park in Hawaii was designed to protect.

In 1949, over the opposition of island hotel operators and tour companies, Senator Noburo Miyake, the chief proponent of the road, sought funds for it in the senate. He was unsuccessful, and the money was diverted to other more practical Kauai roads.

The fluted pali of Kalalau.

Hotel operators opposed the road on purely economic grounds, arguing that tourists wouldn't visit long on Kauai—they could see the island in one day and return to Honolulu without staying overnight. Miyake continued to argue for the road, pointing out that many construction jobs would result and that the road would open up land for subdivision and roadside business.

Through the years many people in power on Kauai looked on Koke'e-Napali as an area for economic development without considering the far greater values of Koke'e Park for public enjoyment of wilderness experience and for protection of the unique natural scenic resources of Napali.

Gross ignorance of park values was revealed in a 1950 territorial legislative resolution calling for a feasibility study of a highway serving northwestern Kauai. The resolution stated:

Whereas other areas of natural beauty such as Nu'alolo, Miloli'i, Kalalau and Hanakapi'ai are relatively inaccessible for lack of good roads, but possess great potential for development, not only for the tourist trade, but also for agriculture, ranching and fishing, this area...could be opened for development if adequate roads were built.

THE PUBLIC WORKS Feasibility Report released in 1951 should have discouraged anyone interested in the road; it said in conclusion: "that the benefits that could be expected by the construction of any of the above roads would not meet the heavy cost of their construction. The construction of roads...would not, therefore, be economically feasible."

The report dismissed the idea of a shore road built along the Napali-Kalalau Trail and beyond to Barking Sands as "too impractical to merit any further consideration."

Joining the opposition with a unanimous Board of Directors' resolution in 1953, the Kauai Chamber of Commerce opposed the projected road as "being prohibitive to maintain" and added:

The Kauai Chamber of Commerce does not feel there is any necessity for having a road completely around the island of Kauai, nor is there an economic need for such a road...tour drive companies would probably lose some business by having a round-the-island road.

But the County Board of Supervisors, faced with increasing unemployment on Kauai in 1954, saw the projected road as an excellent make-work project using public funds, and they justified the destructive road, saying:

The route would open an area of 120 square miles for ranching, truck farming, fruit orchards, sugar and pineapple, with substantial portions of the area suitable for cattle ranching.

They argued it would lead to construction of hotels in the Koke'e and Napali area, and stated further that "forest reserve areas designated as part of the park system may be leased to individuals for commercial development." The military value of such a road was also mentioned, and it was pointed out that "during World War II military authorities had seriously contemplated a similar road to facilitate troop movements."

Ten thousand dollars was advanced out of the Territorial General Fund for construction of a Kokee-Haena road "by prison labor."

THE HIGHWAY DEPARTMENT'S survey crew followed the bulldozers in a classic "push and go" clearing operation, uprooting portions of the only native forest on Kauai that remained untouched by fire or cattle. Ohi'a lehua and ancient koa trees were felled with no public protest by the division of forestry, administrators of the park, or citizen organizations on Kauai.

The forest had no apologist to defend it and died under the onslaught. In eight months the money was gone and the bulldozers were mired. A swath of destruction four miles long ended in the quagmire of Alaka'i Swamp. Men could do no better against the combined resistance of Kauai's finest forest, 200 inches of yearly rainfall, chilly fogs, and slippery clay soil.

Upon further statements by Public Works that the project "does not appear to be economically feasible because of its high costs," requests for additional money were refused. "Miyake's Folly" went no farther.

The damaged ridge above Kalalau has now eroded and dumped ancient topsoil down the walls of the valley, exposing the saddle between Kalalau and Waimea canyons to possible breakthrough. These and other scars of the abortive roadway are apparent to anyone visiting Koke'e, but some feel the lesson is still to be learned by those who are in power on Kauai.

Not all of Kauai's public officials appear to appreciate the great spiritual value of Kauai's scenery or to understand that it must be protected. The road and commercial development of Koke'e will remain a threat as long as Kauai's politicians fail to see the danger of unlimited economic and tourist industry growth.

The danger to Kauai's unique island environment is no longer from sugar and ranching, but from the fastest growing industries of all—construction and tourism. It is not yet time to be unconcerned about a possible Napali road. Work on the road will be renewed whenever a politician thinks the tourist industry needs a road around the island. □

Pu'u Pihea, on the east wall of Kalalau, rises above trade wind clouds marking a tropical air inversion layer.

The Military Invades the Forest Lands

*The Kokee forest, profoundly altered but still
beautiful, was invaded by the military, and the Kokee
foresters faced one of the greatest threats to their
wilderness.*

HIGH-RANKING OFFICERS of the Hawaii Air National
Guard's air defense command visited Maui Island in
1959 and spoke of job opportunities, economic development, and payrolls in a series of well-planned meetings
with service clubs and business leaders throughout Maui. Their
job was to soften resistance from conservationists and gain
support from the community for their request to construct a radar
system high on the 10,000-foot rim of Haleakala Crater in
Haleakala National Park. Secretary of the Interior Seaton,
speaking for the National Park Service, said "no." Despite im-
passioned pleas of its importance to the national defense and
protection of Hawaii from enemy attack, no military radar was
constructed on Maui.

Shortly after the Maui incident a similar team of Air National
Guard officers appeared on Kauai. The Deputy Commander of
the Hawaiian Air Defense spoke to forty civic leaders at a June
luncheon in Lihu'e, asking their support of his efforts to obtain a
site for expansion of Hawaii's early warning radar network,
which, he said, would also include Oahu and Maui, "to monitor
all aircraft entering the Hawaii Air Defense identification zone."
He again emphasized the money to be spent and the new job
opportunities for Kauai residents. Many Kauai businessmen
voiced unqualified support for the installation, without asking the
location, although rumor placed it in Koke'e State Park. In Honolulu, park supporters objected, but were met with arguments that
the installation was important to national defense and with assurances that it was only a temporary measure.

Unknown to supporters and opponents alike, the site had
been already selected by the Air Force five months earlier. In
official, unpublished correspondence were statements by the
Corps of Engineers that "plans called for long-term operation of
the station" in the Kauai mountains.

Without seriously questioning where the site was or if there
would be infringement of park values, the Commissioner of
Public Lands granted right of entry for immediate start of the
project, and the National Guard began construction by winter of
1959. When the early spring visitors to Koke'e arrived, the
entrance to Kalalau Lookout, offering the most magnificent
panoramic view in all Hawaii, was slashed and desecrated by a
monstrous radar dome and array of communications antennae.
The continuous whine of electronic equipment pierced the silence of Koke'e and destroyed the once-peaceful solitude and
wilderness environment of Kalalau.

Very much later, on September 1, 1965, the State signed a
lease agreement with the Air National Guard for the eight-acre
radar site at Kalalau—six years after the facility was constructed
and placed in operation. The 65-year lease specified that "all
structures and signs shall be so designed and placed as to

detract as little as possible from the natural beauty of the surrounding area." It was a little late.

Koke'e Park had no Secretary of the Interior to object. No
Koke'e Park official had ventured to say "no," despite a feasibility
report in which alternate suitable sites on Kauai were named and
mapped, all meeting the Air Guard requirement of an unobstructed northern sweep from a high elevation. The alternate
sites had no paved access road, however, and the Air National
Guard was apparently unwilling to spend funds to construct their
own access road to build at a site less harmful to natural scenic
beauty and public areas of Koke'e State Park.

HAWAII'S FLEDGLING State Park system welcomed its
first director, Richard Dunlap, in 1960. He was greatly
disturbed at the destruction along the rim of Kalalau
Valley and at Kalalau Lookout, and when the Air National Guard
began planning its annual field training at Koke'e, and requested
the exclusive use of organized group camp and housing facilities, Dunlap expressed concern and said in no uncertain terms
that "the primary purpose of these facilities…are to accommo-
date people who come to the park for recreational purposes."

A year later, Haruo Shigazawa, a State Land Office employee,
learned that the Guard was planning to construct a tropospheric
communication facility next to their radar station at Koke'e. In a
hand written memo to Dunlap, he pleaded that no commitment
be made at that time on negotiations for a proposed 65-year
lease to the Guard, because the area they were proposing for
the facility "includes a portion of Kalalau Lookout—the most
significant recreational feature in Koke'e Park."

Hirano Cook, head of the Board of Land and National Resources, opposed the request in a 1963 letter to the Army
Engineers. It was the first time in anybody's memory that a high
Territorial or State official had challenged the U. S. military in
Hawaii. Cook explained the importance of Kalalau Lookout as
"The principle recreational feature of this park" and asked that
"adequate consideration be given to our park plans if military
construction is absolutely essential." In subsequent discussions,
it was disclosed that some of the military problems were financial
and they could not afford to build long access roads to other
sites. However, Cook insisted that every possible alternate location should be explored, and also suggested that the twenty-
acre site be reduced in size so that any military expansion within
the site would not be near the Lookout.

After thinking it over for one year and three months, the Air
Guard decided the "absolutely essential" tropospheric facility
was not needed on Kauai.

It was only a temporary victory for Cook. A second radar
facility was being planned for Kauai. The Pacific Missile Range

In Alaka'i swamp, a vast garden in a rain forest atop an island mountain.

people, who already had space-tracking facilities on Hawaii and Oahu islands, announced that Kauai was being considered for a permanent tracking station to support Project Mercury. Commander Albert W. Hayward, Pacific Missile Range representative, diverted anticipated objections in a release to newsmen on October 28, 1959, asserting that "if Kauai is chosen, the Mana area will be the site." On December 9, Governor Quinn, in a public statement, also reaffirmed that the tracking station would be at Mana, near Barking Sands.

The military had long ago learned that the hand is quicker than the eye, and while publicly pointing to Mana, their engineers were conducting test borings in the Koke'e forest by the middle of November and had concluded electronic tests even before that date.

WHEN THE NAVY first approached the Division of Forestry for a right of entry permit to drill test borings, they refused to reveal the location, saying it was "somewhere on Kauai in the mountains, so just sign the permit." It took almost thirty minutes to find out it was in Koke'e. When asked why Koke'e was chosen, they said nineteen other sites met the site criteria, but Koke'e already had a road and was a developed area. The Navy representative added, "When we are finished, we'll use the facility for recreation cabins and a swimming pool." The military requested exclusive use of 95 acres of park and the Koke'e Park headquarters area all in fee simple. They also mentioned in passing that all private cars and visitors would be banned from Koke'e while the tracking facilities were in use. Rear Admiral Solomons said the 95 acres would provide "minimum space" and were required "to support the Pacific Missile Range in its contribution to the national defense program."

Wayne Collins, head of the Forestry Division, was shocked at the Navy's attitude and received Governor Quinn's support in opposing the uncompromising demands, which amounted to confiscation of Koke'e State Park.

Meanwhile, Admiral Jack P. Monroe, Commanding Officer of the Pacific Missile Range, appeared at Koke'e to inspect the tracking station site, and said the control building would be on Halemanu Hill, overlooking Waimea Canyon. He also affirmed that the "station will be permanent," and spoke glowingly of the $800,000 construction cost and fifty full-time employees.

Collins efforts at compromise were delaying the project, and two weeks later, newsmen still reported that the Navy was looking over "prospective sites." George Siu, acting Land Commissioner, visited Kauai and said, "The State intends to do everything in its power to cooperate with the Navy in establishing the proposed installations...the plans would be an assist to Kauai's economy...This department will see that local interests are protected, safeguarding the forest reserve and preserving the natural beauty of the area for tourists and local people."

Yielding to Collins arguments in support of Koke'e Park's integrity, the Navy agreed that the tracking station only needed 16 acres instead of 95, and that it would be unnecessary to take over the ranger station or close the road. Collins had saved the park, but not without serious losses. Halemanu hill, ancient camp site of the feather collectors and once overgrown with wild

tropical vegetation, was now a leveled acre, sprouting revolving corkscrew antennae for NASA sightseeing.

Parks Director Dunlap sent a long list of damages to the State Land Office, saying, "The installation of the NASA facility resulted in unnecessary damage to recreational values and park improvements which could have been avoided." He specifically blamed "excessive tree trimming and removal of trees in the installation of electric power service...lack of screen (and) or excessive clearing of tree and shrub growth to achieve operational requirements." Hundreds of endemic koa trees, seedling sandalwood, and mature planted exotics had been chainsawed down along several miles of park entrance road by power line construction crews.

Dunlap did not last long as Director of State Parks. His letter was filed and forgotten, and he returned to the mainland. The State Land Office failed to recognize or adequately support his belief that "if military installations are necessary in our parks, they should be located, constructed, and maintained on the basis that fair and just consideration be given to park values." It was a fair enough request. Few would disagree that this could be well accomplished by coordinated planning from the very beginning—including site selection.

THE NAVY CONTINUED encroaching on Kauai forest reserve and park lands. In the winter of 1964, Navy helicopters again buzzed over Napali-Kona forest reserve on what appeared to observers as reconnaisance flights over enemy territory. Occasionally, they landed on isolated ridges and installed portable electronic antennae and technical gear, generally folding everything up and flying off before dark. Surveymen were seen taping the winding dirt road atop Makaha Ridge. Checks with the Territorial Forester revealed that no entry permits had been issued to anyone. Tom Tagawa, staff assistant to the State Forester, advised the Kauai forester to "stop trespassers from continuing further work." The Navy was notified and belatedly requested an entry permit.

The Navy letter must have been hand delivered with great urgency, for on the very next day, the State Board of Land and Natural Resources approved right of entry to the Navy—for surveys only. Regardless, the Navy began clearing Makaha Ridge immediately for construction of radar towers for the complex remote instrumentation facility, heedlessly bulldozing lands of the State forest reserve and the conservation district, land within the area recommended by the Secretary of the Interior for a Kauai National Park.

Kauai forester Ralph Daehler requested that, "If the military must install equipment in the forest reserve, it is my hope that it can be located at the end of a narrow ridge, such as Ka'aweiki, where it will least interfere with ...recreation." Neither the Navy nor the Land Board listened. It was the same story all over again. Despite objections of the Kauai forester, this time supported by Honolulu conservationists, the military was not to be stopped. Even personal pleas to the governor to investigate alternate sites were of no avail—it was argued that the project was in the national interest, and anyway, work had already started. Even Jim Ferry, Chairman of the State Land Board, when asked about the possible damage to Napali, shrugged his shoulders, saying,

Uluhe fern grows a design in the Koke'e forest.

"There is nothing I can do," although at the time a lease had not yet been granted by the Board.

AT THE REGULAR December meeting of the Board of Land and Natural Resources, the Navy's Makaha lease request was discussed (no public hearing was required). Richard Cox, Chairman of the Conservation Council's land committee, testified that the "Council feels that such installation in the area will be aesthetically undesirable," and urged that suitable alternate sites be investigated before proceeding. Staff members of the Division of Forestry in attendance sat in silence, never mentioning the letter of their Kauai colleague opposing the site and suggesting that other sites be considered.

The Chairman of the Board said that he "personally visited the area recently and...the proposed location is rather barren and won't deter the hunting or forestry activities in the area." The Navy representative affirmed that the radar facility would be "below the top of the main ridge" and would not harm the scenic beauty of the area. That was enough for the Board. At the fall of the koa gavel, they unanimously approved the lease. Unknown to the Board, at the very time they were meeting bulldozers were already at work, shaving off the entire top of the lower ridge and pushing soil down the sides of adjacent Makaha Valley. The new lease specifically prohibited "waste, strip, or spoil" and specified that measures must be taken to "prevent damage to...geological features and related natural resources." The Navy had not waited to read the fine print.

Hawaii's Vice President of the Federation of Western Outdoor Clubs wrote Secretary of Defense Robert McNamara, suggesting that the Makaha project be relocated on a ridge less damaging to Koke'e State Park.

The Navy replied for Mr. McNamara, with assurances that the "location was chosen after careful technical study because it is in sight of the airfield and is high enough to overlook and therefore operate effectively with the underwater range just offshore." Rear Admiral V. G. Lambert expressed confidence that the construction "will in no way mar the natural beauty of Makaha Ridge," though it already had. He ignored the fact that forester Daehler's alternate proposal for Ka'aweiki Ridge would have placed the facility even closer to Barking Sands and the underwater range while still maintaining the desired altitude. A subsequent exchange of letters between the Navy in Washington and concerned conservationists in Honolulu only revealed further strangeness in Navy logic. When it was suggested that the Navy combine its facilities with the NASA Koke'e tracking station, saving millions of dollars in construction costs, Admiral Lambert claimed that an "inversion layer" prevented use of radar above 2,000 feet, yet the joint Air Force-FAA radar facility atop 4,500 foot Mount Ka'ala on Oahu experienced little difficulty. When questioned, several FAA radar operators said they had no particular problems with any "inversion layer" and were mystified that anyone would consider it a problem in Hawaii.

All arguments failed and the Navy rolled on The private contractor for the Navy quickly proceeded to construct supporting buildings and erected two sixty-foot radar towers on windswept Napali. The strong, bold cliffs, rising majestically 1,500 feet above the blue sea, once a landmark for the early Polynesian voyagers to Hawaii and later probably the first land seen through the ocean haze by Captain Cook, could no longer be a quiet resting place for hunters or hikers marveling at the vast, unbroken panorama.

The unique natural beauty of the Napali coast, once stretching without pause fifteen miles from Barking Sands to Ha'ena, and viewed from the air by thousands of visitors every year—was irreparably broken at Makaha.

Sunao Kido, Deputy Director of the Land Board, wrote Governor John Burns that "I am satisfied...that this Department has taken every reasonable precaution against any wanton destruction of Hawaii's natural beauty." Hawaii's State Park Director, Joseph Souza, once a ranger at Koke'e, was quoted by Kido as saying "that no work on the ridge is visible from the highway." Kido could have gone further and said that no work was visible from Honolulu.

Rear Admiral Lambert, Chief of the Bureau of Naval Weapons, had the last word on the completed facilities, saying that their "usefulness in the interest of national defense should silence those who find them objectionable." □

THE BRUTAL DESTRUCTION of our landscape is much more than a blow against beauty. Every artist, scientist and philospher in history of mankind has pointed to the laws of nature as his greatest source of inspiration: without the presence of nature, undisturbed, there would have been no Leonardo, no Ruskin, no Nervi, no Frank Lloyd Wright. In destroying our landscape, we are destroying the future of civilization in America.

— Peter Blake

Dam Builders Threaten the Wilderness

*Development of the resource that had made Kauai
beautiful and its agriculture rich, now became an
issue, and the Bureau of Reclamation offered its
help—at an unknown cost.*

SOMETIMES HIDDEN in narrow slots of deep canyons, at other times dropping boldly in thousand-foot falls, Waimea River surged unobstructed to the sea sixty years ago. Wild Hawaiian ducks floated lightly on sometimes frothy, sometimes tea-colored water from Alaka'i Swamp, the river's source. The river scoured the cliffs of Waimea Canyon, and continued seaward, replenished on its way by numerous streams and springs draining clear water from the dike complex within the porous volcanic rock. Great quantities of storm water escaped freely from the wettest land on earth, flowing deep in this, the longest river in the Hawaiian islands.

As the river neared the sea, small diversion ditches carried water into taro patches and as quickly returned it to the river. The river's flow was maintained and neither in winter nor summer did the sand at the river mouth close across the stream. Waimea Village, embracing both sides of the river where it entered the sea, never flooded.

Hans Faye's artesian wells, scattered about the Mana plains, provided ample water for cane irrigation in these early pioneering days. As planting expanded and additional lands closer to Waimea were reclaimed, additional sources of water were required, and Faye investigated the possibility of bringing waters from Alaka'i Swamp, which was at a sufficiently high elevation for gravity irrigation of the Mana lowlands. His ideas were translated into a feasible ditch system by Kekaha Sugar Company engineers, and by 1910 Kekaha completed a small diversion structure at the junction of Koaie Stream nine miles upriver, in the heart of Waimea Canyon, diverting virtually all the summer flow of Waimea River into extensive, newly cultivated cane fields in the Kekaha uplands.

Within a few years after water was diverted from Waimea River, its physical appearance changed markedly. Trees and brush swiftly sprouted and grew in the dry channel when waters shrank to a trickle during summer months. Soil, sand, and rocks slid into the channel in spring freshets, and normal winter flows were no longer sufficient to clear the channel. Once ten feet deep for most of its length, the river became a sluggish, shallow stream, flowing between exposed lava boulders. At the river mouth, where small sailing schooners once anchored for provisions and fresh water in depths of over twenty feet, a permanent sand bar obstructed the river's entrance to the sea. The channel had plugged up. There was no longer a river reservoir to hold flood waters or to keep open a clear passage to the sea.

In 1912, Waimea Village was flooded for the first time in the villagers' memory, when the river overflowed during winter rains. Every year thereafter, the river crested dangerously, causing minor floods and constantly posing a threat to life and property in a village unprepared to cope with the rising waters. Eleven years

after the Kekaha Ditch was completed, Waimea suffered severe losses in the worst flood ever to inundate a Kauai community. An act of man had changed an act of God into disaster.

After Kekaha successfully purchased its power plant and the Waimea diversion dam lands in the 1920 auction, management invested heavily in an elaborate system of small dams, ditches, and tunnels to skim off additional Waimea River water at its source in Alakai Swamp.

Roads were built by hand across Koke'e and into Alaka'i. Camp Ten on Mohihi Stream became notorious as the coldest and wettest habitation on Kauai. With little mechanical equipment, miles of ditches and tunnels were pushed through the rock and clay rim of Waimea Canyon by pick and shovel. The rough construction crews lived on the land, and foraged all of Koke'e for fish and game. Exotic plants were cultivated for food along the surveyed route and allowed to spread wild into the jungle as the tunnel crews advanced. Koke'e cabins were broken into and hunting regulations violated in a lawless atmosphere reminiscent of railroad building in the wild west.

WHEN THE DITCHES and tunnels were completed in 1927, 1,000 acres were added to Kekaha's sugar production by the gravity water system, and work continued on the 1.7 billion gallon reservoir on Waiakoali Stream to hold water sufficient for another 2,000 acres of irrigated cane. The concrete dam core was poured and plans for clearing 100 acres of Alaka'i Swamp for the reservoir site prepared, when visiting senators expressed concern over construction of large reservoirs at the head of Waimea Canyon. They considered introducing bills requiring government approval of plans and specification to protect the residents of Waimea from possible failure of the dam with a reservoir filled to capacity. No concern was expressed for the rare flora and fauna threatened with destruction by sluicing out of Alaka'i Swamp the material for an 887-foot-long earthen dam.

Unforeseen engineering and political delays plagued Kekaha's construction timetable, and the dam and reservoir projects were abandoned because of the short time remaining on the lease. Depression fears postponed work again following the lease in 1938, and war clouds mothballed the project when plans were revived in 1940. After World War II, Kekaha hesitated again, awaiting a new lease, hopefully of longer duration. The delay was fatal to the private project.

Kauai Republican Senator Noboru Miyake introduced a resolution in 1949 memorializing Congress to develop water storage facilities at Alaka'i Swamp for irrigation and production of hydroelectric power. Kekaha manager Lindsay Faye pleaded that if the lease were renewed, the plantation would be willing to con-

Kauai is the only Hawaiian island with rivers, all flowing from the high watershed of Wai'ale'ale, rainiest place on earth.

struct the original irrigation reservoir project with private financing. Faye asked the Territory to grant a longer lease and a subsidy in form of reduced land rental for 15 years.

But the Territorial government, now no longer completely under planter influence, pulled the rug out from under Kekaha in renewing the lease and cancelled all water privileges Kekaha had previously enjoyed. Water development rights were transferred to the Territory and made available to Kekaha under terms of a water license. Fifty years of private water development in Kekaha-Koke'e came to an end as the new postwar politicians moved government into active management of water resources and created the Hawaii Irrigation Authority.

Government control of water could have been a good thing. The government could have established a program of water development in the best interests of the land and of all the people of Kauai, but it did not. Kekaha Sugar's threat to Koke'e and Alaka'i Swamp was nothing compared to the threat soon posed by the U. S. Bureau of Reclamation.

A special Congressional committee of the House Interior and Insular Affairs Committee came to Kauai in 1954 for public hearings and Senator Miyake followed their visit with a letter to Public Lands Commissioner Marguerite Ashford, asking her to initiate an investigation of the possibilities of government participation in an Alaka'i Swamp reservoir. Miyake had apparently forgotten the Territorial law he had authored which specifically limited the Irrigation Authority to projects serving "small-scale farms," except for the right to sell water in excess of the needs of the farms within a project. The 15,000 acres of Hawaiian Homes Commission lands in the mountains southwest of Koke'e offered opportunities for homesteading to small farmers, but would use only a small portion of the water available from a major irrigation project. Officials also ignored the fact that Hawaiian Homes commissioners had no plans for use of its upper Kekaha lands, nor had any investigation been made of their suitability for agriculture. Nevertheless, the 1955 Legislature directed that a study be made for a public irrigation project in Koke'e, although the only known beneficiary was Kekaha Sugar, which for three decades had attempted to construct an irrigation reservoir and dam with its own funds.

FINDINGS OF THE 1957 Irrigation Authority report to Republican Governor Samuel Wilder King should have discouraged proponents of the project. The report stated "that it would not be practicable to incorporate either flood control or hydroelectric power development in the plans for the proposed Koke'e irrigation project," and went on to say that "since the project area is isolated from the Honolulu market, a relatively low cost of production would be required to offset the high transportation costs …There is inadequate information to show that crops can be grown under irrigation in the service area at a sufficient profit to the homesteaders to insure the financial success of a project."

The chief engineer of the Authority did find, however, "that it would be feasible to construct a somewhat limited project to provide the additional supply of water needed for optimum irrigation of cane on the 2,200 acres of government land now leased by the Kekaha Sugar Company."

IGNORING THEIR OWN adverse report, the Irrigation Authority recommended that the Legislature appropriate $250,000 to make detailed engineering and geological investigations of a project they had concluded was economically unsound. Kauai Representative Allen Ezell supported the Authority, and introduced a resolution to make the Koke'e project eligible for Federal funds under the Small Reclamation Projects Act of 1956. The Bureau of Reclamation, ever anxious to expand its sphere of influence, jumped into the act.

Floyd E. Dominy, Commissioner of the Bureau of Reclamation, collaborating with the State Division of Water and Land Development, authorized a "Kokee water project" report. Even Dominy recognized the improbability of any diversified farming on Hawaiian Homes lands "because of the many economic uncertainties and technological problems involved." The feasibility of the irrigation portion of the project was based entirely on the assumption that all the water would be devoted to sugar cane production, assuming, of course, that Kekaha would buy water at the asking price.

The value of the Koke'e dam to Kauai was proven largely illusionary in the report, although Kauai politicians kept up their claims of more jobs, more farms, and cheaper power. In actuality, the project would offer few new jobs, no economically practical small farms, and might actually raise the cost of consumer power on Kauai for the next 50 years.

The hydroelectric power plant was designed to provide power only at peak loads. There would be insufficient water to run the turbines at the design rate for more than a few hours a day without draining the reservoir. Existing steam plants would have to continue to operate and new plants would continue to be built as demands increase. Kekaha would be unable to use all the water at peak flows even in the dry summer months, and the surplus water could only be flushed into the sea. In winter months even less water, or sometimes none at all, would be required to satisfy sugar irrigation needs. To expect Kekaha to pay for water it cannot use would be unreasonable, but it was an assumption important to the justification of the dam.

Cost of hydroelectric power was estimated as being at least equal to cost of producing power with steam generators fired by oil and presently unused cane waste bagasse. It was claimed that the private public power utility on Kauai, would be able to build a conventional power plant at Port Allen using private capital, and supply power to Kauai at a much cheaper rate than proposed in the hydroelectric project.

Flood control benefits would be negligible, and the small farms the dam was supposed to make possible are uneconomic in Hawaii. Oceanic Properties, land development subsidiary of Castle and Cooke, one of the nation's largest food processors, reported to the State Land Use Commission in 1963 that, contrary to general opinion, "Availability of additional land is not a major factor in determining the amount of truck crops now grown or that will be grown in the future." According to Oceanic Properties, "If the 550 acres now used for truck crops on Oahu were fully used,…Oahu could produce all the truck crops it needs for its 1970 population without importing any from the neighbor islands." Oceanic stated that small farmers could not compete with the mainland in growing major truck crops.

The unique environment of Alaka'i swamp protects some of the rarest plants on earth, indigenous to the island of Kauai.

In the entire State of Hawaii, only 1,300 acres are used for diversified farming. Should all the proposed 1,600 acres in upper Kekaha be put into successful truck crop production, by small farmers or by an efficient large agricultural company, it would mean economic ruin to every small truck farmer in the State. It is difficult to believe that supporters of the Koke'e project would advocate something so economically undesirable.

The Bureau figured the benefit-cost ratio at 1.44 to 1.00. Even this low index was obtained by computing power revenues 22 per cent higher than current power rates and adding water revenues from Kekaha Sugar based upon year-round averages—whether Kekaha used the water or not. Either the people of Kauai would pay more for power, or Kekaha would pay more for water. The Bureau would find its benefit-cost ratio at zero and the Federal loan to Kauai a grant unless the people of Kauai were willing to pay more for power and Kekaha accepts lower profits. Neither eventuality appears likely.

ONE HUNDRED and fifty acres of Alaka'i Swamp adjacent to the botanically important Lehua Makanoe bog would be stripped to a depth of twenty feet to provide fill for the proposed half mile long earth dam on Kawaikoi Stream. A six-acre rock quarry blasted from the rim of Waimea Canyon would provide lava rip-rap. A second dam is proposed on Mohihi Stream, deep within Alaka'i Swamp, to divert additional water into a canal one mile long, penetrating untouched swamp country. The proposed reservoir would flood more than 400 acres of the Alaka'i Swamp Wilderness Preserve, and coupled with strip mining for fill material, hauling roads and construction camps, would ruin perhaps one thousand acres of unique American swamp land. The irreplaceable flora and fauna are not represented in the Koke'e project's "benefit-cost" index, and are by no means replaced by the recreation value of a reservoir estimated to fluctuate over 150 feet in depth, denuding the shoreline of all vegetation. Little boating or fishing recreation, in any case, could be enjoyed at the reservoir site which is only a few miles from the wettest land on earth and where rainfall reaches 500 inches in some years.

The Board of Land and Natural Resources set aside 9,939 acres of Alaka'i Swamp as a wilderness preserve on January 24, 1964, yet the Koke'e Water Project Report, released later in the year, does not recognize the preserve's existence. The preserve is an important one. Several species of native perching birds, found only in Alaka'i Swamp, are becoming very rare. Most significant of these are the 'o'o, the Kauai 'akialoa, nukupu'u, and the puaiohi, or small Kauai thrush, all members of a unique Hawaiian family of birds, some of which are nearly extinct. The birds are dependent on undisturbed native forest, and the proposed reservoir site intrudes upon their principal habitat. Recreation motorboat noises and the dieback following land clearing and trail building in the tropical jungle may result in total loss of birds found nowhere else on earth. Mountain streams such as Kawaikoi and its tributaries, are used year-round by the koloa, a rare native Hawaiian duck, which might find a fish-stocked, boat-filled reservoir quite inhospitable.

Citizen opposition and bureaucratic bumbling unable to separate the various needs of corporate sugar, Hawaiian homesteaders, and the apparent desire of the local utility to generate electrical power for profit doomed the Alaka'i hydroelectric project. It just wasn't possible to justify such an elaborate boondoggle on such a small island. The politicians gradually gave up, but the threat continues, for the people of Kauai may still be paying the highest electrical power bills in the nation.

Increasing concern by local residents over the adverse consequences of expanded resort facilities, and accompanying population increases, have generated proposals to reduce energy needs and limit tourist growth on Kauai. Residents along the Hanalei shore have consistently opposed reconstruction of the obsolete highway bridges serving north shore communities, some of them narrow one-way bridges still partially collapsed from the 1946 tsunami. They are well aware that new bridges and widened highways will mean new hotels and tourist crowds.

Conservation activists have opposed lengthening the Lihue airport runway, successfully stopped major resort development at Maha'ulepu, and come within 36 votes of making the existing 40-foot building height limitation a law without any possibility of variance.

Should the people of Kauai eventually succeed in halting tourist growth, future demands for an Alaka'i hydroelectric project will substantially lessen, but the threat to Kauai's unique wilderness will not entirely disappear, for mineral exploration teams have mapped extensive areas of bauxite and titanium deposits on the high plateaus above Waimea and Hanapepe towns. The varied colors photographed by tourists in Waimea Canyon identify mineral deposits that could bring about the canyon's destruction.

The bauxite deposits are low-grade ore and at present of little commercial value--so long as bauxite deposits elsewhere remain abundant and available. Should demands for aluminum increase and overseas bauxite ore reserves decrease, strip mining of Kauai's low-grade ore may become practicable. The state of Hawaii holds the mineral rights to underground Kauai. Plans for undertaking strip mining operations have already been prepared by the Department of Planning and Economic Development in collaboration with large multinational mining corporations.

One possible mining scenario calls for the sluicing of strip-mined ore from the plateau above Makawele, across Alaka'i swamp in large pipes to Hanalei, using water from a Kawaikoi stream dam and reservoir. This frightening proposal also calls for construction of a high dam flooding the entire Wainiha valley to generate electrical power for an aluminum smelter on Hanalei bay. The shallow bay would be dredged to allow ocean-going freighters to load refined aluminum metal directly from shoreside wharf facilities. The proposal would create a multimillion dollar industry for Kauai, with hundreds of new jobs, and would provide a tax base sufficient to satisfy every county government need.

It would also destroy Kauai as an island place for living. □

Wai'alae stream

I HAD BEEN on Kauai just four years when the doctor told me to report to the hospital. It wasn't just the bronchitis, there seemed to be a more serious complication, too.

During those four years, I had moved from being a stranger on a small island to being a known quantity; from being stared at, to being given my place in the pattern of people…"You know, Jean Holmes the newspaper wahine."

But was being accepted "belonging?"

When the clerk in the admitting office asked, "…and who is your next of kin?" my stomach twisted. That meant "who will claim the body?" and except for my teenage son, there was no next of kin within 5,000 miles.

I named a next door neighbor to be contacted "if", climbed into the clean white hospital bed, clasped my hands on my chest and prepared to die bravely…and alone.

First the flowers started to come, the beautiful blossoms of Hawaii from somebody's yard and the exotic mainland imports. My room soon looked like a florist shop.

When the first ten dollar bill fell out of an envelope I was taken aback…after all, in my scheme of things you only sent money to poor people, charity cases.

A Japanese friend explained that this was completely proper. It was considered a "loan" and I would be expected to do the same if a member of my extended family fell on hard times.

It seemed that the Island conspired to keep me company. A rainbow of races…Hawaiian, Japanese, Chinese, Filipino, Portuguese and Haole, and the beautiful results of inter-racial marriages…sat around my room until I was almost relieved when the nurse shooed them out at eight o'clock and I could drop smiling off to sleep.

When I (surprise!) got well, and was sent home to the inexperienced care of my 15 year old son, the warmth followed me there.

He never had to cook a meal. From my bed I would hear the footsteps on the stairs and the knock at the back door…"Here's some chuck…or chicken…or stew…or pudding…for your mother."

One night, as I scraped the last of the custard from the bowl, happy tears ran down down my cheeks and dripped into it…because I knew I do have next of kin…all over the Island of Kauai.

They are funny-kine people. They insist on knowing all about you…your affairs of the heart, body and pocketbook. But that means they can rejoice in your happiness, share in your sorrow and help out either way.

Like the woman who, hearing my car had a major breakdown, brought over hers, dropped the keys in my hand and said…"Use it as long as you need, we have two."

They are quick to needle you. Like the man who laughed loudly at a party, calling attention of all to this "Haole too poor to own a washing machind"…and quick to help. It was his pick-up truck that delivered a used washer (free) to my door the next day.

"We're getting a new one…"

Like any family, we squabble among ourselves, but are quick to defend each other from outsiders.

I'm glad I have the people of Kauai as my "next of kin."

— Jean Holmes, Editor
The Garden Island

Hanalei bay on Kauai's north shore. Highrise hotel construction has been discouraged by destructive tsunami's and obsolete highway bridges have been preserved by citizen activists intent on protecting the rural environment.

WE HAVEN'T REALLY been measuring any of our natural resources well because many of us have let a conventional wisdom get in the way of our thinking. We have settled for short-range predictions projected from a knife-edge instead of a base. Our perspective on what technology can do for us, and to us, is perilously limited. What man and technology have achieved is so spectacular that it preempts our attention; it lets us forget the most important element of all in what makes natural beauty something worth photographing and writing about.

That important element is life. The life force, the unbroken living chain that extends back to the beginning of life on earth, that from the long-ago beginning on down to each of us has never failed to reproduce itself well and move on. That force, in two billion years, also has produced a miraculous complexity of living things, each as dependent upon the others as a cell of one part of our body is dependent on those of its other parts. That life force has produced organic wholeness, and Robinson Jeffers would have us "love that, not man apart from that."

Do we? Or do we take that organic wholeness apart, tinkering with it and losing the parts, simplifying it without even asking how dangerous to us it may be to simplify it? Compulsively we take a natural piece of land, with all the species that magically convene on the surface we see, rising from below the surface out of all the life forms we can't see or know, and we order this miracle to reduce itself to a single crop. Instead of respecting the natural succession of cotton or cane, or peanuts or pine, we simplify the biology without really knowing what we are doing to the land over the long run that man really must count on.

With our spanking new toy, technology, we have already done more to disrupt natural things in our lifetimes than were disrupted by all the living things, including man, in all previous history. Whereupon, we freely predict that we can go on the way we're going, doubling our numbers every thirty or forty years, doubling our appetite for natural resources every decade, holding ourselves before the world as a model for all others, not thinking through, evading the truth that if the rest of the world obliterated resources at our speed, resources would go twenty times as fast as they are now disappearing. Can we go on this way, worship growth, confuse it with progress, and get on with it?

I don't think we ought to try it much longer. If we think we can get away with it because science will save us, we haven't been listening carefully enough to the scientists wise enough to admit their own limitations. They, you, we, need to volunteer for the good war, the war against myth, the battle of words for the earth; we need to do the deeds that will rebuild the respect for the earth that our forbears had and our children might like a chance to discover.

—Dave Brower, President
Friends of the Earth

Awa'awapuhi valley, a crack in Napali, ends against a waterfall where the narrow valley is only wide enough for a person to stand.

The Heritage of an Hawaiian Ethic

What the botanist considers an ecological disaster
the visitor considers it the most beautiful landscape
ever seen.

FOR ALL THE neglect and abuse of its past, the land of Kauai remains the most beautiful in Hawaii. Between the dunes of Barking Sands and the summit of Mount Wai'ale'ale, the wettest spot on earth, lie one hundred square miles of spectacular parkland: sea cliffs dropping half a mile to the Pacific Ocean surf; hidden valleys a thousand feet deep and a rock throw wide; rolling hills covered with red-blossomed ohi'a lehua; delightful walking trails at the edge of Alaka'i Swamp—a wilderness brightened with rare plants and with bird songs heard nowhere else in the world.

Dramatic variations in weather occur within the area. The five thousand foot summit of Mount Wai'ale'ale on the eastern boundary averages 500 inches of rain per year, and one year 950 inches were recorded, yet only seventeen miles to the west, arid Barking Sands receives a scant 20 inches. The vegetation varies accordingly, and the hundred square miles is an exotic garden from around the world.

The gracefully fluted cliffs of Napali rise directly from the blue Pacific to elevations of 2,000 to 3,000 feet. The spectacle of the coastline culminates in Kalalau Valley where the stone ruins of Hawaiian villages, ancient at the time of Captain Cook yet still populated fifty years ago, lie buried beneath lush tropical growth. The nearly vertical cliffs enclosing the valley are alternately revealed and obscured by shifting clouds carried on tropical trade winds, and occasionally the Specter of the Brocken appears on the moving mist.

The broad sweep of white coral sand at Barking Sands ends abruptly at Polihale Springs where the pali rises from the sea. For fifteen miles Napali continues, sliced sharply by deep, narrow valleys, many inaccessible except from small boats in the summer, or by helicopter. Deep volcanic browns are broken only by the occasional green of grass, until the more verdant amphitheater of Kalalau provides water for the bright leaves of mango fruit and *kukui* nut. Farther on, at Hanakapi'ai and Limahuli, a misty jungle softness darkens the trees clinging to steep walls. At Hanakoa a two-thousand-foot string of white water drops from the pali top and then twists along the valley floor beneath groves of mountain apple trees.

The heart of the land is Alaka'i Swamp. Streams from the swamp rise and fall with the rain but pour all year long over rocky waterfalls into Waimea and Wainiha Canyons. Alaka'i is twenty miles of wilderness bog, rich in species of sedges, violets, and lobelias found nowhere else in the world.

Three species of birds; the Kauai creeper, the akialoa, and the nukupu'u survive in Alaka'i. They persist precariously, in constant danger of extinction from environmental alteration and introduction of alien plants. In the deep gorge of Waimea Canyon, the rare koloa maoli, or Hawaiian ducks, float on the slower pools, where noisy females can be heard quacking above the sound of the water. Once common throughout Hawaii, the small brown duck is now seen only in Waimea Canyon and on Niihau.

In Waimea Canyon the island's geological history is exposed in desert colors of orange-red cinder and brown decomposed lava, interrupted by bright green gulches of kukui. Waimea River is a sparkling chain 2,500 feet below the canyon rim. Along the canyon edges grow the Kauai greensword; on drier slopes grow the native white hibiscus tree, the only fragrant hibiscus. Thirty endemic lobelias can be found, including one with unusual blue flowers, and sandalwood is returning. Palms are scattered throughout the native forest, along with passion fruit, wild plums, and apples. Introduced trees grow well, including Japanese pine, cypress, silver oak, and redwood. Wild boar and goat bring the thrill of wildlife to the quiet jungle and windswept pali, and mokihana is here to make into the most fragrant lei of all.

The natural beauty of Kauai is only part of its appeal. The legends and stories of Hawaiian oral literature have endured here and on the other islands as few American Indian legends have endured in the continental United States. The aboriginal population of the islands, where land was limited, was heavier than anywhere on the mainland, and the land is more strongly imbued with the spirit of the native people. On Kauai, where the land is wildest, the native tradition is most intact. Every valley, cave, mountain and stream has its story.

ONE OF THE CAVES at Ha'ena was the home of a dragon. He was a dragon with taste, and he chose a good spot. From the base of the Ha'ena cliffs the view of the beach is excellent, and the beaches at Ha'ena are among the most beautiful in the Pacific. The producers of *South Pacific* shared the dragon's delight in them and chose Ha'ena as the location for their movie.

There are three caves at Ha'ena. The "dry" cave is at the base of the vertical cliffs behind Ha'ena beach and its entrance is almost hidden in a forest of Java plum and kukui trees. It's a huge cave with a broad arched roof and vaulted chambers, and it would seem an ideal shelter from evening rains. Campers have discovered, however, that mosquitos from all over Kauai use it for that purpose. Sleeping in the rain is easier on the skin.

Once, long ago when savage battles were fought between rival chiefs of Kauai, an entire native army is said to have been imprisoned in the cave by hostile soldiers, who walled up the entrance. The prisoners were slowly starved to death, except for a young warrior who discovered a small opening through the cave roof and escaped to find aid. He returned too late. His former companions were all dead and the enemy was celebrating with savage orgies on the grounds of the present Ha'ena county park pavilion.

Farther along the narrow country road to Ke'e Beach are two "wet" caves. On the floor of the first is a shallow and innocent pool. On the floor of the second, another pool, this one the home

Sisal blossoms rise above the Kalalau valley floor, covered with introduced mango, orange, java plum and lantana.

of the dragon. The water of this second pool is perfectly transparent and reflects the dim light from the cave's entrance, but it was not always so. Before 1898 the pool was covered with a yellow scum, a scum formed of the scales shed from the dragon's back. The dragon had its lair in the depths of the cavern, and anyone foolish enough to swim in the cool water would surely be seized. Today the scum is gone. The surface has been clear since the annexation of the Hawaiian Islands by the United States. The dragon, a loyal one, could not endure the domination of an alien race, and it departed for a far island where no white man has ever set foot.

The Hawaiian explanation for the red water of Alaka'i Swamp is as colorful as the explanation for the yellow scum at Haena Cave. I heard it on my first trip into Alaka'i.

My guide on the trip was Fred Taniguchi, a Robinson ranch cowboy and Japanese-Hawaiian son of Puakini, a famous Kauai guide familiar with every ridge of the Napali-Kona forest reserve. Loading our gear in Taniguchi's front yard at Waimea, we started off at dawn and spent the first day on horseback. It was a hot, dusty ride to our overnight stop at the old CCC camp on Wai'alae Stream. Here Kauai Forester Duval had planted the first redwood trees. They formed a small grove near the main building and were easily 75 feet tall, casting long shadows in the late afternoon sun. We expressed mixed feelings at finding the huge strangers, already many times taller than endemic ohi'a lehua trees, in the midst of our Hawaiian forest. Our thoughts were quickly diverted, however, when one of our group discovered exotic plum trees nearby, the branches bent almost to the ground with ripe purple fruit. Few native Hawaiian trees taste as good as the exotic introductions.

T HE NEXT DAY we were up again in the chilly dawn air, and started out on horseback into a forest filled with birds and huge ohia. We crossed and recrossed Wai'alae Stream, which flowed full with red-brown water from Alaka'i. Occasionally, I reached down and plucked red thimble berries from along the trail or aimed my camera to snap masses of white ginger. Their deep fragrance stayed with us long after the blossoms disappeared from view and we began to climb the steep switchback trail out of Wai'alae Valley into Alaka'i Swamp.

I asked Taniguchi how much farther we could go on horseback and he said we would know when we had gone far enough. We plodded onward into the swamp, the horses sinking deeper into the gray muck. Suddenly my horse lunged forward as he stepped across a fallen tree. His front legs dropped into the clay without meeting resistance and his belly hung over the vine-covered log. Taniguchi dismounted, slopped his way over to my frightened horse and said, "This is far enough." I felt like a horse myself as I stumbled on foot deeper into the swamp, sinking with each step in the quagmire of a thousand years of rain.

One of the myraid small streams flowing from the top of Wai'ale'ale through this area has one of those unbelievably long Hawaiian names; *Ehaehaekamanuekanealohikealemainei-kawai,* which in our language means, "Tear of the bird, Kanealohi, the water is rippling." It refers to the tea-colored, sometimes reddish-brown water draining from Alaka'i Swamp. The scientific staff attached to the State Division of Forestry

believes that the red color is caused by the 'ama'uma'u fern, growing in many areas of Koke'e and Alaka'i. The Hawaiians have a more reasonable explanation. They tell the story of Princess Komalio, daughter of the high chief of Waimea, who was loved by Mano, a demigod. She failed to appreciate the honor and spurned his attentions. He kept at his courting, however, and one day he appeared in disguise at Waimea, in a canoe, announcing that he was a chief from another island. Even then she did not favor him, as she disliked his shifting and unsteady gaze—a "bad eye".

F AILING TO WIN her confidence, Mano decided he would have to use force to get her to his mountain lair. He changed himself into a great bird, and flew to the home of Komalio in Waimea. Finding her alone and sleeping in the garden, he seized her in his powerful talons and carried her to his cave near the headwaters of Wai'alae Stream. As he changed back into his ordinary form and lifted her sleeping body toward his lair under a waterfall, several drops of water fell on her face. She awoke, became frightened, and started to struggle. Mano lost his temper, killed Komalio, and buried her body by the side of Wai'alae Stream.

Since then, every time it rains in Alaka'i Swamp, the water runs through her grave, and the streams beneath it are red with her blood until they drop over the rim of Waimea Canyon.

There are two rocks between Nualolo and Awa'awapuhi Valleys that have an origin as unhappy as the origin of Alakai's red water. The Hawaiians were a lighthearted people, but they appreciated tragedy, and most of the phenomena of their world had tragic explanations.

The two rocks are high on a talus ridge above what used to be the trail. They somewhat resemble humans climbing up the narrow ledges, and indeed they were once human, or superhuman. Their story is this: One of the powerful demigods who ruled the island, Naiwi by name, lived on the tops of ridges along this coast with his family, which included two children. One of the regular duties of the children was to climb down the cliff to the beach, fill their calabashes with water from a spring famous for its sweetness, and return to the top before dawn. The children, like most demigods, went out only at night, for daylight was fatal to them. They were children, however, and sometimes loitered on the way, playing pranks along the pali or stopping at some convenient flat spot for a game. One morning they became so engrossed in their play that they failed to notice the brightening sky to the east. When they finally saw it, they scrambled up the ridge as fast as they could climb, but succeeded only in reaching a point on the ridge just below the sheltering home caves. As they climbed over the last pinnacle before reaching the friendly shade of the mountain they were overtaken by the first deadly rays of sunlight, and instantly turned to stone. The two children stand on the pali today, the undelivered calabashes of water still on their backs, a lesson to all children on heeding the warnings of their parents.

The Hawaiians left more than just stories and ghosts on Kauai—they left tangible things; temples, house platforms, and terraces. Of sensible design to begin with, they are in disrepair now, their edges and angles softened by time and weather.

A grove of Kukui in Awa'awapahu valley frame one of the two children of the demigod turned into stone with a calabash of water still on their backs.

There is nothing in them out of harmony with the land, and coming upon one while walking on Kauai is one of the fascinations of the island.

There is one temple, on Mount Wai'ale'ale, that still receives offerings. I camped near it several years ago, eager to try out a new tent I had bought in a mountain shop on the mainland. Wai'ale'ale, the rainiest place on earth, would be the ultimate test for my tent.

VISITORS TO THE SUMMIT of Wai'ale'ale usually use Ke'aku cave for shelter, and I ate dinner there, but the cave is always cold and damp and I was happy to brave the rain and pitch my tent. I crawled in for a cozy night, listening to the rain splattering lightly against the cotton tent walls, confident that I was camping in as wet a place as anybody had ever camped in before. I listened as the rain increased in intensity, and felt around anxiously for any leaks. The rain falling on the taut sides became louder and louder. The tent was soon like the inside of a bass drum. The noise became almost unbearable, but I was not about to leave the tent, and although I did not have a moment's sleep that night, not a drop of water entered the tent.

Near where I pitched camp on the summit, the Wainiha River, which flows into the Pacific Ocean on the north shore, has its source in a small lake. Held sacred by the early Hawaiians, it is hardly a real lake, only thirty feet in diameter and two feet deep in a rainstorm, which is almost always. The lake bottom is composed of small pebbles and sand and the water is clear, in contrast to the surrounding muck and stubby grass. Near the lake is a small temple platform of hand-fitted rock about ten feet square. It is the heiau of Wai'ale'ale, to which the Hawaiians of all classes once toiled from Hanalei and Waimea to pay homage to the gods of the woods and mountains.

The head gods of the mountain, like the Ha'ena dragon, may have departed in disgust, but Wai'ale'ale still dominates the island. For me it has always been, even more than the swamp, the most fascinating place on Kauai. Nowhere in the world is weather—the primeval power of cloud and rain—so dramatically on display. Camping on Wai'ale'ale is an experience like no other—not even approached in the Cascades of the northwest or in any other wet place in the continental United States.

Ke'aku Cave is the only dry place within a dozen miles of Wai'ale'ale. Perched high on the side of a clay cliff near a small stream that lower down becomes the Olokele River, the small cave, not high enough for a standing five-footer, is deep enough to stretch out in, though tenants must roll up their sleeping bags to cook dinner. The cave is one mile and three hours from the Wai'ale'ale summit, which though it is not the highest point on the mountain, is the most comfortable high point. Kawaikini peak, ninety feet higher and three-fifths of a mile south is too small and slippery to stand on.

The small stream is a hundred feet below the cave, but water needs are easily satisfied. We held a pan outside the cave entrance into the steady rain and filled it up in minutes with fresh, cold water. Far back in a dark corner of the cave is a crumbling wood calabash, undoubtedly brought here by a Hawaiian many years ago. We found an old rusting ship's lantern resting on the smooth, worn surface of the cave floor, but it fell into small pieces when we picked it up.

A native lapalapa tree stretches its slender branches across the cave entrance, shivering as its leaves catch the light breezes. The rare tree, growing only at high altitudes in Hawaiian swamps, has white wood that burns when it's green. Hula girls in the old days were called olapa because they wiggled so much.

The tree offers a good perch for island birds, and curious over the rare visit of humans, they flock there. Birds seen nowhere else in the world are silhouetted against the overcast sky, perched on the mossy branches, singing unfamiliar calls and seemingly oblivious to the rain pouring from everything. Most noticeable is the bright scarlet 'i'iwi bird with its long curved beak, a beak especially suited for gathering nectar from lehua and the rare lobelia blossoms. Occasionally a green leaf will flutter gracefully away—an unknown bird camouflaged for the rain forest. The 'akikiki or Kauai creeper chirps constantly in the cold, wet air, enjoying the rain and human visitors alike.

ONCE I GOT LOST on a photographic expedition in Alaka'i swamp with Dick Davis, who was carrying most of my camera gear. We had been chopping our way through the jungle, finding no sign of the summit trail to Wai'ale'ale, when Dick suddenly stopped swinging his machete, and called me to look. Straight ahead of us was the fresh path we had cut not an hour before. We had tramped in a circle and were lost.

Our predicament was serious, and we immediately climbed a tree to see what there was to see. The sky was overcast and misty. Every tree was the same height and all we looked into were the upper branches of more trees. The old boy scout trick of finding north from the side of the tree growing moss didn't work here. Moss several inches thick grew all around the slender branches I held on to, and when I squeezed a new branch it squirted like a clam.

We held still, watching the sensitive lapalapa respond to the slight breezes, and after a half hour we agreed on the direction the wind was blowing. We stared at the rain clouds for minutes at a time, turning our heads to what we thought was the brightest spot in the darkness. We didn't notice any birds on the ground, but as we waited silently in the tree they flew over to look at us, perching within arm's reach on the wet branches.

Acting upon a unanimous vote, we decided the direction we should go, and set out again. We had a map but no compass, and the map was virtually worthless because we were not quite sure where we had started out from. Eventually we stumbled upon a stream we had encountered on our way in, and we retraced our steps back to camp. We returned considerably more aware of the danger of overconfidence in the Kauai wilderness.

Wai'aleale and Alaka'i swamp present a more unusual challenge than common mountains of rock and ice. Camping on it can be trying, but the epidermis is waterproof, and once you're used to it, rain can be refreshing. Bill Hardy, who climbed the mountain 22 times between 1911 and 1920, clearly couldn't get enough of Wai'aleale's rain on his face or mud between his toes. For the old Hawaiian priests, for Bill Hardy an numerous Kauai residents and visitors who have made their way to the wettest place, Kauai's high mountains and hanging valleys were indeed very special places.

Trade wind clouds fill Kalalau valley with foggy mists that often clear into sunshine and blue sky for visitors willing to wait in the constantly changing weather at the rim lookout.

It is a land that deserves special recognition and preservation, a more certain protection than the territory and state have demonstrated in past years. Continued desecration of the wilderness environment of Koke'e and Napali has been stopped more often by citizen pressure from the people of Kauai than by any expressed concern of responsible authorities in state park and forestry agencies. When the parks division planned improved picnic grounds and a new lookout into Waimea canyon at Pu'u Ka Pele, the State Land Board noted to allow use of the site for helicopters to land and take off over the Waimea rim. The acting chief of parks who objected never did become anything more than "acting." Not until 1979 did citizen pressure bring about regulation of Napali sightseeing helicopter flights, something the helicopter companies themselves find important to continued operations that respect the wilderness environment.

BLACKBERRIES, pink poha and passion fruit vines still threaten the Koke'e forest. Trees that provided shade and beauty ten years ago are dead branches today—if they exist at all. Blackberry thickets in the Bird Park of Hawaii Volcanoes National Park were completely eradicated by the park service many years ago.

The mountains and pali lands of Kauai need the protection of a great national park. The problems of providing more opportunities for recreation and wilderness experience to increasing numbers of tourists and new residents, while protecting Kauai's irreplaceable natural assets, are not being met by state government agencies. Sufficient dedication to wilderness values by successive administration, the legislature and tourist industry are seriously lacking.

Citizen activists doing their best to preserve the natural beauty of Kauai would have found the National Park Service able working companions. But in 1967, when I introduced the proposal for a Kauai National Park, which was to include all the high mountains, deep valleys and the sea cliff shore of Napali, the Kama'aina sugar planters and cattle ranchers rose in anger. They would have none of the federal government controls—they would not release their control over "their" island, and they successfully opposed the concept of a national park for Kauai. Corporate landowners did not take to the idea of protecting the wilderness "forever." What if, in the future, they wanted to use it?

Secretary of the Interior Stewart Udall was invited to Kauai by national park proponents to personally view Kauai's wildlands. On his first day on Kauai, he walked up to the Kalalau lookout railing, barely visible in a late morning fog, and waited, while I explained the typical Kauai mountain weather and how the sky would clear. "Wait a little". He did wait, and on cue, as if the Sierra Club had made arrangements, the clouds soon were blown aside to reveal a magnificent rainbow spread completely across Kalalau valley. It was unreal, even to us who had seen the view many times. Udall watched enthralled as the view continued to clear, revealing all of Kalalau and Napali. He turned to me, excited by what he saw and exclaimed, "Get me the proclamation! I'll sign it right now!"

A sugar planter standing nearby, blanched and scowled at me. I think at that moment the campaign to stop the national park began. Only public lands were being considered for the park, but to the planters of the time, state land was their land to control. It always had been that way and they would tolerate no change.

What the sugar planters and ranchers said is what happened on the Kauai of 1967. They promised the sugar workers extra union benefits if they opposed the park. They easily turned the hunters against the park, saying there would be no more hunting on Kauai, despite the fact that feral goat and pig were causing widespread damage—there would be more hunting within the national park, not less. They told the owners of illegal cabins in the Koke'e forest that their cabins would be confiscated. Taro farmers on the north shore were warned that their farmlands would be condemned.

It was a shameful campaign of deceit that I tried to answer, but Kauai's Chamber kept me quiet. When the Chamber of Commerce agreed to hear me at the next annual meeting, their largest dues-paying member said he would resign unless the invitation was cancelled. It was. An Ele'ele radio station taped an interview with me about the park, announced when the tape would be played, and then cancelled the program when several businessmen warned that they would otherwise cancel their advertising.

SUPPORT WAS widespread among those who understood how a national park would permanently protect the beauty of Kauai. When I visited Kauai, I drove a free rental car, stayed without bills at the best hotels, ate at many local restaurants without receiving a check. Small merchants on both south and north shores voiced considerable support for the national park proposal, but few would allow their names to be used. They feared retribution by those who opposed the park. Kauai was a small island and still a company town. It was best not to publicly go against those who owned the island.

"The Koke'e — Napali scenic lands are a unique and valuable asset of the state and nation," said Udall. "I consider this one of the most important and significant areas proposed for addition to the national park system during the nearly five years that I have been Secretary of the Interior. It is one of the crown jewels of the islands and would be a superb addition to the national park system."

It was not to be. The Kauai national park proposal died for lack of support from a community that in 1967 was still a sugar plantation town and which behaved accordingly.□

Covering the sand, a wave changes into froth and fades away at Black Pot beach, where Hanalei river enters the bay.

What is the use of a house if you haven't got a tolerable planet to put it on?

— Thoreau

Far back inside Nu'alolo-'aina, this hanging valley above the surf on Napali bends around a corner in the earth and becomes a mystery that even Hawaiians declined to explore. Kukui grows comfortably in the ancient grasses and recent lanatana.

Kalapaki Beach

KALAPAKI, on a cove of Nawiliwili bay, was the beach house of the William Hyde Rice family, and in later years the home of Grace and Charles Rice, who wed in 1899 and lived at Kalapaki for many happy years. They traveled to Honolulu only to attend territorial legislative sessions with Representative, then later, Senator Charlie Rice. The land is part of the original Kalapaki ahupua'a of Kauai King Kaumali'i.

Two Hawaiian families also lived in the valley. The Kepeka Keoma Ah You family, in a small green house on an old kuleana land grant, and another family, whose old tutu was reputedly a kahuna, in a home far inside the valley, separated from the main house by two taro patches next to Mrs. Rice's lily pond. Mango trees grew behind the taro patches, and mullet and moi on the Kalapaki table came fresh from the nets of Pokoka and Uhuhu, grandsons of the old tutu. They dried their nets on the horizontal branches of kiawe trees growing next to the beach. Keoma Ah You was coachman for the Rice family, driving matched carriage horses named May and June. The Rice home needed little from outside the valley, with their own chickens, three Jersey cows, a small orchard and two vegetable gardens, where in later years monkey pod and tamarind trees were planted by Rice's ranch hands. Raw coffee beans were kept in the scullery back of the large kitchen, brought out and roasted in the oven in a shallow pan and then ground in a hand-turned grinder.

Living at Kalapaki was always a gracious event. Formal dinner parties in the 19-room beach home, attended by close friends and ranch and plantation associates, were elegant affairs with guests dressed in black-tie dinner jackets and long evening gowns. The table was set with Dresden china and Venetian glasses, monogrammed damask tablecloths and other napery, with centerpieces of water lilies from the pond. There were white-suited waiters and Japanese maids in kimonos, wine glasses and candlelight.

There were always many courses, often with fruit and avocado to start, followed by clear soup with sherry, then fish or lobster from the Ha'ena reef in creamed mushrooms and Rhine wine and probably, roast beef or even wild ducks that Charlie Rice had shot. Salad would follow, made of leaf lettuce from the Kalapaki garden, served with oil and vinegar. Dessert was generally Grace Rice's favorite—her specialty of sherry-soaked ladyfingers and macaroons with strawberries and thick cream fresh from the newfangled milk separator brought on the ship from Honolulu.

After the death of Grace, Charlie remarried, and his wife Pat carried on the traditions of plantation living at Kalapaki. The porte cochere echoed constantly with the banter and laughter of friends driving to the house in the newest automobiles on Kauai or gathering together for a horseback ride on the family ranch at Kipu.

The magnificent home and everything in it was destroyed early on the morning of April 1, 1946, when a destructive tsunami generated by a major earthquake in Chile struck Hawaii without warning. A series of giant waves 30 to 40 feet high flooded Kalapaki and returned to the sea, sweeping into Nawiliwili bay splinters and debris from the Rice home. Not a wall was left standing. The yardman was killed instantly by a coconut log driven through his chest.

Pat Rice had just finished nursing her six and one-half-month old-son, Robin, when she heard the commotion outside. She saw the second and largest wave approaching and ran for the baby's crib as the wave roared into the house. The room filled with swirling water as she grabbed her baby and was swept helplessly seaward on the retreating wave, with household furnishings and broken walls, into a turbulent sea of struggling animals and floating wreckage. Twice she was swept back ashore only to be carried again into deep water. Robin was pulled away by the surging water, but she grabbed him back and riding the crest of the third wave was finally far enough inland to where Pat could cling desperately to a cluster of ha'u branches at the lily pond and stop herself from again being sucked into the harbor. Completely exhausted, but alive, she collapsed into the helpful arms of the two Ah You boys, who carried her to high ground. Charlie rushed home to find her and Robin safe.

Many years later, scouting for a hotel site on Kauai, Dudley Child, president of Inter-Island Resorts, chose Kalapaki as the ideal beach on which to build his new multimillion dollar Kauai Surf Resort. He bought the land from Charlie Rice. Only one small house remained on the property. Badly in need of repair and another coat of green paint, it stood forlornly between the lily pond and the beach. Living in the house with her grandson was an elderly Hawaiian woman, Mrs. Kepeka Keoma Ah You. She was the last of the old Kalapaki.

Mrs. Ah You soon found herself directly in the middle of Hawaii's newest jet-age development: a sentimental picture of the old Kauai of simplicity and charm and the new Kauai of tourism and progress, and she refused to move. Bulldozers surrounded the tiny green house, flattening the low hill nearby where Charlie Rice's home once stood, now the site of a nine-story hotel of gray concrete slowly rising above the valley. Carpenters banged away in their work on a coffee shop and cocktail lounge next door where a backhoe steadily dug away, excavating for the hotel swimming pool.

She took little notice of the intruders who moved in on her quiet life. Once a bulldozer moving earth on the hill above dislodged a boulder that bounded down straight toward her house, stopping in the middle of her carefully tended backyard. Workers ran down the hill to apologize, but Mrs. Ah You smiled back with unconcern, saying "There was no harm done." Another time she complained to the workers, "In my icebox, water all come out. No stay cold. You spoil all my kaukau. Your machine use all the electricity." It seems the single power line into Kalapaki was not enough for the hotel builders and her refrigerator.

Mrs. Ah You was born at Kalapaki. She was married in the green house and raised her 17 children there, in the shadow of the Rice home next door. To everyone who asked she emphasized, "I am going to stay right here. If I left, where would the family go when they come to visit? I was born here. I grow up here. I marry here. My children born here. I stay here."

But soon it was apparent to all that Mrs. Ah You could not live very well in the middle of a hotel, and she eventually agreed that it would be best for her to move.

The people of Kauai surf bought her kuleana land and paid to pick up her house with a crane, exactly as it was because she did not want a new house. It was moved to the top of the highest hill above the new hotel, where it remained for several years, alone against the blue sky with clothes occasionally fluttering on the wash line in the morning sun. She had the best view of all.

One day a returning visitor to the hotel noticed that the Hawaiian lady was no longer watching the afternoon sky from her lanai. Next month the house was gone. Today only the lily pond, kiawe and tamarind trees remain to remind visitors of another, older time in Hawaii. □

often repeated the observation by Thoreau, "What is the use of a house if you haven't got a tolerable planet to put it on?"

Kauai ceased being a company town when the tourists arrived. The importance of sugar to the island economy decreased in direct proportion to the number of new hotels. Growing with the expanding tourism were associated service industries: rental cars, restaurants, entertainment and island fashions. As sugar dollars contributed less and less to island paychecks, the political influence of sugar management waned—sugar planters no longer had much to say about anything. Few listened. Once-influential kama'aina's were ignored, while community activists, public defenders and young politicians of a different breed assumed positions of influence and moved the island politic into new directions reflective of increasing environmental concern.

In the late sixties, transient "hippies," packaged tour groups and NASA discovered Kauai. NASA was watching satellites orbiting overhead, occasionally dropping them on the moon; the tour groups were just looking; and the hippies wanted to "drop out" where it was warm.

As Kauai passed from the days of sugar barons into a contemporary American community, an active middle class appeared where none existed before. It assumed prejudices of its own while taking up newly acquired leadership roles in the evolving community, while shucking the images and the practices of a company town. The new "establishment" was quite proper in its measure of citizen behavior—it proceeded to welcome the immigrants spending money and those building the hotels, while harrassing transients and short-term visitors who professed a desire just to live on the land and emulate what they thought of as old Hawaiian lifestyles. When several transient families (unmarried and long-haired) overstayed the time limit of county park permits, they were arrested for vagrancy and given ninety day jail sentences, to be suspended if they left the island.

North shore resident Howard Taylor felt it was deliberate harassment, hardly reflecting the traditional aloha spirit apparently being eroded by people a little different than Kauai islanders. Taylor had purchased seven acres at Ha'ena to subdivide and build a future home, but his plans were stopped by condemnation proceedings to acquire the property for a state park. He offered the use of his land as a temporary home to get the visitors out of jail and personally located the area where the visitors could live, marking the boundary with a can of spray paint. Thirteen temporary residents left the Wailua jail and moved into the forest at Ha'ena. Within two years, perhaps sixty people lived on the land soon known as Taylor camp.

A new kind of subdivison grew on the site. County planners denied the new residents building permits for conventional housing on the ground, so they took to the trees, constructing elaborate tree houses within the upper branches of a Java Plum forest, a grove of the trees that were introduced into Kauai many years before by plantation foresters. Some houses were supported on long bamboo poles, with wood siding and windows facing the sea. Most inhabitants enjoyed cool tradewinds on living platforms without walls, protected from rain by yards of transparent plastic draped beneath the canopy of leaves. It was

a shadowless environment in the soft green twilight of day, and when enhanced with often-smoked pakalolo (marijuana) grown in nearby valleys, the village in the sky must have been a very sensual living place. Inhabitants enjoyed a self-proclaimed religion called the Church of the Brotherhood of Paradise that welcomed all believers (even atheists), shared experiences in God, the sun and mystical power of the pyramids. While general nudity and free sexual relationships prevailed, women who wished to live alone were never bothered by amorous males, and community order was maintained by a spontaneous understanding of the need for common sense and good judgement. There were no locked doors in Taylor camp, because there there were no doors. Personal possessions in private quarters were seldom disturbed, contrasting with increasing petty crime in the established community outside, which considered Taylor camp a somewhat bizarre settlement.

AS THE SELF-STYLED "proper" citizens in town attempted to reconcile their need to enjoy nature by fishing on weekends or taking the family for a picnic in the park, but never too far from their automobile or the all-electric kitchen, the long-haired mainlanders talked themselves into believing they had abandoned the trappings of urban life; but it was not so. Residents of Taylor camp considered themselves to be living "close to the land" in an idyllic escape from the world outside, but they never ventured too far away from the general store. When Taylor camp was finally abandoned, twenty-six stripped cars were found in the parking lot. A joint archaeological field dig by the University of Hawaii and the University of Illinois at Urbana-Champaign turned up evidence that inhabitants had ignored the abundant sea life and devoted little time to growing their own food for subsistance.

Ha'ena had been occupied over many generations by native Hawaiians and a comparison of garbage thrown out by the two cultures proved to be quite informative. In the old garbage pit, excavators found opihi shells, "fish-bone, pig and dog bone and even fish scales." The Hawaiians had no Ching Young store down the road in Hanalei. They lived by the land.

Garbage piled up by the new inhabitants proved them to be quite dependent on a money economy—profits from pot and welfare and unemployment checks. Excavations from the Taylor camp period produced considerable glass and metal trash, rotten tent fabric, metal grommets, a tab top probably from a beer can, and an empty sardine tin that had been packed in Maine. So much for living on the land by haoles.

In many ways, Taylor camp is an intriguing symbol of the transition underway in postwar Kauai, of the struggle to live from the land and at the same time to preserve the land and traditional property rights. The cultural conflicts inherent in the immigrating mix of mainlanders conflicted with tourists who stayed for only a few days and with wealthy couples buying limited land intending to stay forever and inflating prices in the process. All gathered together on an island stage already crowded with local people rapidly becoming average American middle-class citizens.

Problems multiplied quickly for those who considered further population and tourist growth anathema to Kauai's future. A *Honolulu Advertiser* editorial, written in 1959, following comple-

Sunset at Ha'ena, the Bali Hai of Hollywood's South Pacfic.

Deborah Kapule's Ponds

THERE ARE FEW coconuts in the high palms bordering Hawaiian Queen Deborah Kapule's ancient fishponds at Wailua. They might fall and hit a tourist on the head. The grass beneath Deborah Kapule's great coconut grove, said to be the largest and oldest in Hawaii, is cut short and trimmed regularly by power lawn mowers. Instead of piled heaps of ripe brown cocnuts beneath each palm, ready to be husked for copra, there are tin gallon cans containing a portion of coconut husk soaking in kerosene. They have been prepared for the nightly torch lighting ceremony conceived by Coco Palms hotel's manager Grace Guslander. Every major hotel in Hawaii now presents a torch lighting ceremony inspired by the first ceremony began here many years ago by native hotel employees clad in red "malos," running from torch to torch. The conch shell still sounds at Coco Palms every evening at sunset.

Kapule's fishponds are no longer used for raising mullet, and transient ducks eat the floating lily pads; but thousands of tourists who sleep beneath her coconut grove, within sight of her old fishponds, are probably beneficiaries of her hospitability and worldliness.

She was born at Waimea, where Captain Cook landed on Kauai. Her father remembered seeing the British explorer, and in later years she gave birth to her own world traveler, George Humehume, who lived several years in New England, returning to Hawaii with the first missionaries. Her casual liaisons with a variety of men distressed later missionaries, who suspended her from the church. She was six feet tall and weighed perhaps 300 pounds, quite appropriate for royalty in a race noted for imposing stature.

After Kamehameha II abducted her husband, King Kaumali'i, and his son by a previous marriage (then a paramour of Kapule), she moved to Wailua where she married a devout church worker and lived in the grand manner of an island chieftess. The coconut grove was enlarged and fishponds constructed on the grounds; "the first pond for taking the saltiness from the fish, the second for sweetening them, and the third for fattening the mullet." Her several thatched huts offered hospitable overnight accommodations for missionaries and travelers who enjoyed her excellent table, which always included fresh fish from her ponds and beef from purebred cattle grazing in the nearby coconut grove.

Upon her death, the missionary newspaper of the time reported her loss as "deeply felt by her people, among whom her influence for good was very great." She died in 1853. Her gardens and fishponds remain.

tion of Kauai's first high-rise, stirred up considerable debate by suggesting that "other appealing (resort hotel) sites are at hand, from Barking Sands and Koke'e to Hanalei." Many opposed the idea of a national park for Kauai simply because it would become another tourist attraction. In ensuing years proposals to lengthen Lihue airport's runway and to build new highways and new bridges were fought with varying results. The new jet hydrofoil service from Honolulu was opposed and the legislature-supported interisland auto ferry was condemned resolutely as a potential disaster to Kauai, opponents' arguing "Who wants all of Oahu's automobiles on *our* island."

SUBDIVISION ORDINANCES were tightened and it became increasingly expensive to build. A contemporary account listed Kauai as one of the least desirable places to retire in America because electrical, food and building costs were so high. All subdivisions were required to install wiring underground, and the local planning commission added more and more restrictive conditons to every subdivision request, responding directly to their constituents' concern. New construction continues, but at a considerably slower pace compared to the rest of Hawaii.

During a meeting of the Kauai planning commission where a new interim zoning ordinance was under discussion, it was urged that Kauai adopt building height limitations. Commissioner, now state representative, Tony Kunimura suggested that new buildings be limited to the height of coconut palms. No one knew how high the typical coconut palm was, so a survey was made of coconut palms around the island. Average height was found to be forty feet, although some older palms were eighty feet tall. Accordingly, the interim zoning ordinance limited building heights to forty feet plus the roof. It was the usual Kauai way of doing things.

It became awkward to challenge the Kauai citizens, who seemingly wanted to save everything. Anything might happen and often did. When the local savings and loan company announced its intention to cut down a hundred-year-old banyan tree on Rice Street to build a new office building, the local Mokihana Club formed a committee to save the giant banyan. The company relocated its building to retain the tree and the women's committee made ready to dissolve themselves when the state highway department published plans to widen the airport road into town, a proposal that would require destroying one of the largest false kamani trees in Hawaii. The Mokihana women went to work again and stopped the highway department. Before disbanding this time, the committee decided to list all the largest and most significant trees on Kauai, to put everyone on notice that politicians and developers should not even think of removing certain trees. They became part of an Arborist Advisory Committee to compile a list of the most important trees on Kauai. The county council passed the Exceptional Trees Ordinance, making it illegal to even touch certain trees without government permission. The Kauai women, trying to save one tree, had saved an island of trees.

Then the state-financed Hawaii Visitors Bureau came under attack by individuals who wanted to abolish the famed tourist promotion agency. The HVB office has repeatedly demonstrated its effectiveness in persuading major motion picture producers to film on Kauai. *South Pacific* is really Kauai in the minds of thousands of tourists who want to see the beach where she "washed that man right out of her hair."

When the residents of Kanoa Estate lands at Niumalu learned their rented homes were to be sold out from under them for newly legal condominium apartments, a new kind of militant community association evolved, made up of residents who simply refused to move from what they considered to be their land to live on—regardless of what the deed said. It was at Niumalu where the Hawaiian people fought their first major land use battle.

Even Amfac, when it was called American Factors and whose every desire was once the final word on Kauai, ran afoul of determined low-rise proponents when Amfac applied for a variance to build an eight-story hotel at Poipu beach. The planning commission cut the request to six stories, hoping to silence opposton, but opponents went to court, continuing to insist on four. After considerable legal skirmishing Amfac finally agreed to keep its new hotel at the established coconut palm height.

Those who wanted to keep Kauai's urban profile low did not forgive the planners for having granted Amfac a variance for six stories, so petitions were circulated to make forty feet the law of the land, to make it impossible for appointed commissioners to grant a variance for anything higher than forty feet. At the ensuing island-wide balloting, the initiative lost by only thirty-six votes, providing an excellent indication of how the Kauai electorate felt about their island.

The "low-rise" committee did not fade away, but wrote a bill for the council to introduce which would have the same effect as the failed initiative—to limit the planners' perogatives. It passed the council by a simple majority, but was vetoed by county mayor Eduardo Malapit. He didn't think it was necessary, because there had been, according to Malapit, "no abuses" of the planning commission's power to grant height variances.

COUNTY DECISIONS accurately reflected intensifying environmental concern for Kauai and for the even split in popular support on conservation versus development. Councilwoman Jo Ann Yukimura spoke for the environment when she challenged the mayor following his veto, claiming "Had Amfac not withdrawn its request for a six-story hotel at Poipu which had been granted the planning commission, other resorts in the area would have asked for the same privilege. And since we have no criteria on which higher buildings are based, the next request could have been for six-to-eight stories, and the next eight-to-ten."

Yukimura claimed that "That only reason Amfac had withdrawn its request was because of the huge public outcry, and the public should not be required to do the work of its elected and appointed officials. Maybe not today," she prophesied, "but

Uluhe fern, considered a pest by foresters, smothers native plants in thickets that are easier crawled under than walked through. Uluhe is why so many of Kauai's mountain ridges are always green.

someday there will be a low-rise law to protect the life-style of Kauai."

The threat is real. The speculators are waiting in the wings. On the mountainside of Nawiliwili Bay, 1,396 acres of conservation-zoned land sold in 1966 for $24,000. In 1978 it changed hands for $700,000. In 1979 the land was posted in Realtors' Multiple Listing for $7,500,000! At the time, it was carried on the county tax rolls at an assessed $14,000 with taxes of $210 a year. Someone apparently thinks Kauai's environmental concerns are only a temporary aberration that will soon fade away.

THE ENVIRONMENTALISTS win some and lose some. They stopped the largest hotel and condominium development ever proposed on Kauai, the hotly contested project at Maha'ulepu, then lost their campaign to stop another large condominium project at Nukoli'i. But the planned condo site at Black Pot on Hanalei Bay became a county beach park. The beautiful shoreline and miles of wildlands and beaches from Ha'ena to Miloli'i, including Kalalau and Napali, became Napali Coast State Park, perhaps the largest state park in the nation. Many environmentalists feel that Kauai is ahead in the struggle to save her beauty.

The three lots that brought about the Poipu beach controversy and inspired S.O.B. T shirts, were purchased by the county for a beach park. The old bridges beyond Hanalei are still frail and narrow, still stopping tour buses and trucks and giving highway engineers cause for anguish. They give most of the Hanalei people reason for joy.

Three of the bridges — the lacy truss bridge across Hanalei stream and the Waioli and Waipa bridges beyond Hanalei town—have been declared eligible for the National Register of Historic Places. Hanalei Bridge is the oldest surviving metal truss bridge in the islands, and the two smaller spans are early examples of flat slab concrete engineering. Any move to tear down or alter the bridges will now require appropriate review by state and federal historical agencies.

Two of the flat slab bridges were undermined and partially collapsed by the destructive 1946 tsunami. They remain, tilted awkwardly, yet still in use, because the highway department refused to repair the bridges — state engineers insisting upon building wider bridges with wider highways connecting them. The current director of Waioli Mission House in Hanalei, Barnes Riznik, reflects the consensus of Hanalei, saying, "If the road is improved and the bridges replaced, the pressures for development will increase." The threat of another tsunami flooding the flat Hanalei shore has undoubtedly discouraged many developers with grandiose plans. The forces of preservation have done well in partnership with the forces of nature.

Kauai residents earn a fine living from visitors, and Kauai's continued hospitality and "aloha" attest to a comfortable relationship. There is no reason why a satisfactory combination of a limited number of tourists and of residents cannot be found: a combination of needs that will keep Kauai a "garden island" for living and dreaming.

THE DRAMATIC HISTORY of Kauai is still seen in the unique tropical landscape, which when combined with the unique island life-style, can surely be preserved for everyone, while still allowing new cultural sparks to light and glow is the island environment.

Kauai island is, in many ways, a "national" park for everybody, while remaining the backyard of those who live on Kauai. This magnificent island treasury of human and botanical impact, covering over one thousand years, is here for everyone to observe and experience in awe, even as the island continues to change, for each visitor to Kauai leaves behind an ecological footprint that may well be visible in ways that will not be known even one hundred years from now. These words and pictures may kick loose some innovative thoughts from visitors and residents who do not intend to change the future of Kauai, but who nevertheless will leave a lasting mark on this Hawaiian island in the Pacific.□

A MUCH YOUNGER Hawaiian than I…explained that he was taught by his parents and grandparents that whenever the family went to the mountains for ti leaves for a small party, they would strip the ti leaves but leave the core of the plant to reproduce. If the leaves were for a large party, they would break off the leafy portion of the ti plant and plant a portion of the stock of the broken-off piece of ti. This practice was necessary not only because the immediate family will again need the ti leaves, but also the neighbor, the other person, will need the life-giving ingredients of the ti plant.

The basic vestige of our heritage of being concerned for others is the inner human beauty that Captain Cook referred to when he described a populace with behavior patterns so free from reserve and suspicion which today we term, inarticulately, as our "aloha" spirit, a spirit of acceptance and concern for others.

In our present democratic society, we must bring people together in a closer relationship of concern for each other and thereby enhance…the ancient sense of the inner beauty of old Hawaii — a balanced relationship with nature.

— Myron Thompson, Trustee
Bishop Estate

A waterfall without a name streams down the cliffs of Napali, where it bathes transient campers before disappearing into the sands of Kalalau beach.

Waimea canyon. The middle of Kauai where the earth shows what it is like inside; where water from Wai'ale'ale drops from mountaintops and begins flowing to the sea; where tropical forests evolve into desert cactus; and tourists and residents stand side by side to see the view. The visitors have flown a thousand miles to see the spectacular backyard of the island residents living in Waimea and Kekaha towns.

Hawaiian Glossary

THE EARLIEST KNOWN list of Hawaiian words is in Captain Cook's account of his explorations, compiled in 1778, the year he first landed at Waimea. The words were his phonetic idea of what the sounds looked like, based on his knowledge of the Tahitian language. They are quite different from what we read today; Atoui (Kauai), Wymoa (Waimea) and Eneeheeou (Niihau).

Fifty years later the first missionaries from New England created their own written version of Hawaiian. Using the missionary Hawaiian, we have compiled another shorter list, mostly of place names to assist in pronunciation and to enable readers to better understand a beautiful language, which for the first time since the days of Hawaiian royalty is being taught in island public grade schools.

Reverend Lorenzo Lyons wrote in 1878 that the Hawaiian language "is one of the oldest living languages of the earth, as some conjecture, and may well be classed among the best…The thought to displace it, or doom it to oblivion by substituting the English language, ought not for a moment be indulged." We agree. It is for this reason that anyone can quickly recognize Kama'aina islanders, for their conversation will be well sprinkled with Hawaiian words fondly adopted over the years.

The Hawaiian language, compiled by the missionaries after their arrival in 1820, has changed little, but dictionaries and the printed form have changed from time to time; in this book we have used the presentation that most clearly reveals the correct spelling and proper way to pronounce even the most complex words. Glottal stop marks are used throughout the text, but for reasons of clarity in reading, we have not used the hyphen; however it is included in the glossary. All that we know is derived from the *Hawaiian – English Dictionary* by Mary Kawena Pukui and Samuel H. Elbert, and *Place Names of Hawaii* by Mary Kawena Pukui, Samuel H. Elbert and Esther T. Mookini. Both are published by the University Press of Hawaii, Honolulu.

It is not possible in one paragraph to properly explain how to pronounce Hawaiian, except to suggest the reader try to pronounce words the way they are spelled. Pronounce each vowel as a separate syllable, with the accent on the next to last syllable. Vowels are pronounced like *a* in above, *e* in bet, *i* in oily, *o* in sole, and *u* like in moon. Give *w* a slight *v* sound. To further aid in pronouncing words with multiple vowels, the glottal stop is included, making the sound similar to the *oh's* in English *oh-oh*. Hyphens are not pause signals, but indicate separate syllables. Each entry is pronounced as a single word: Awa-'awa'puhi= Awaawapuhi. Being able to properly pronounce Hawaiian greatly enhances the pleasure of reading about Kauai.

It is not always possible to provide a precise definition of Hawaiian place names, because their meanings often are not possible to understand in the context of current usage. But certain names give us a hint of some ancient relevance, as in Hanapepe, which has been translated as "crushed bay." A more reasonable explanation might be: *hana,* "to make," plus *pepe,* "baby". Perhaps a Hawaiian chief had stopped there for a night.

Āe'o	Hawaiian stilt (*Himantopus himaniopus knudseni*).
Ahupua'a	Hawaiian land division extending from the mountains to the sea.
'Akialoa	Hawaiian honeycreeper (*Hemignathus obscurus Gmelin*)
'Akikiki	Hawaiian honeycreeper (*Loxops maculata bairdi*).
Alaka'i	The high mountain bog in central Kauai. Leading the way.
Alakoko	Fishpond constructed by the legendary Menehune in one night.
Ali'i	Hawaiian royalty.
'Ama'u	An endemic genus of fern (*sadleria*).
Anahola	Land section along Kauai's east shore.
'Anianiau	Small, yellowish green Hawaiian honeycreeper (*Loxops parra*), endemic to Kauai.
Awa-'awapuhi	Narrow valley on Napali. Ginger root.
'Ekaha	Bird's nest fern.
'Ele'ele	Village on the south side. Black
'Eli	An individual land parcel lived on by a commoner.
Hā'ena	County beach park on the north shore. Redhot love.
Hale-manu	Mountain area on Kauai. Bird house.
Hāmākua	Coastal area on the Big Island.
Hanakāpī'ai	Nearest valley to Ke'e on the Napali trail.
Hanakoa	Small valley on Napali.
Hanalei	Area on Kauai's north shore. Crescent bay.
Hanamā'ulu	Place north of Lihue. Tired from walking.
Hanapēpē	River and small town on south side.
'Ie'ie	Climbing vine (*Freycinetia arborea*).
Ka'ala	Highest mountain on Oahu island.
Kā'awe'iki	Valley in the Waimea district.
Ka-lā-heo	Rural area on the south slopes of Wai'ale'ale. A proud day.
Ka-lalau	Largest valley on Napali. Straying foolishly.
Kalapakī	Beach near Lihue. Site of Kauai Surf Hotel.
Kālepa	Ridge along the shore south of Wailua river. To trade.
Kāne	Man.
Kapa	Cloth made from bark.
Kaua'i	(Most Hawaiians pronounce the word with a glottal stop.)
Ka-wai-kōi	Alakai swamp stream. The flowing water.
Ke'ā-kū	Dry cave near the summit of Wai'ale'ale.
Kē'ē	The beach and cliff at the end of the road beyond Hanalei. To keep away.
Ke-kaha	Caneland on Kauai's southwest shore. The place.
Kiamanu	Collectors of birds, gathering feathers for the capes of ali'i.
Kīhāpai	The commoners own small farming patch.
Kilohana	Volcanic hill northwest of Lihue. Lookout point, the best.
Koa	Indigenous tree used by Hawaiians for canoes. Bold and fearless. (*Acacia koa.*)
Koai'e	Stream draining Alaka'i swamp. (Named for the koa tree.)
Kohala	Land district on the Big Island, Hawaii.
Kōke'e	Largest state park in Hawaii. To bend.
Ko-loa	District on Kauai where the first sugar plantation was established in 1835. Still a working plantation.
Koloa-maoli	Native Hawaiian duck (*Anas wyvilliana wyvilliana*).
Konohiki	Headman of a land division ruled by a chief.

Kukui	Indigenous Hawaii tree of many used by early Hawaiians. Candlenut tree (*Aleurites moluccana*). Light.
Kuleana	Land parcels owned outright by native commoners as a result of small land grants by the king.
Kumulipo	Source of Life.
Lehua-maka-noe	Miniature 'ohi'a lehua tree found in the Alaka'i bog (*metrosideros collina spp. polymorpha var. pumila*).
Lele	To jump. A flea.
Līhu'e	County seat of Kauai. Cold chill.
Liko	Leaf bud.
Liliko'i	Passion flower or purple water lemon (*passiflora edulis*).
'I'iwi	Red Hawaiin honeycreeper (*vestiaria coccinea*).
Loulu	Native fan palms (*Pritchardia*).
Lumaha'i	Beautiful beach beyond Hanalei.
Mā-hā'ule-pū	Rough coral limestone shore east of Poipu. Falling together.
Māhele	Division of land.
Maile	Native vine used for leis (*Alyxia olivaeformis*).
Mākaha	Ridge at the west end of Napali. Fierce.
Maka-weli	Land area on the south side of Kauai. Fearful features.
Mamo	Black Hawaiian honeycreeper (*Drepanis pacifica*). The yellow feathers were the most prized for the featherwork in royal capes.
Mānā	Dry, westernmost place on Kauai. Supernatural power.
Manene	A kind of plantain found only on Kauai (*Plantago pachyphylla var. kauaiensis*).
Menehune	Legendary small people who worked only at night.
Milo-li'i	Beach and valley on Napali. Fine twist as in coconut sennit. Ocean current swirling like twisting cord.
Mōhihi	Steam in Alaka'i swamp. Variety of sweet potato.
Mokihana	Mountain tree (*Pelea anisata*) found only on Kauai. Lei for the ali'i.
Moku	Large island districts ruled by high chiefs.
Mo'o	Lizard.
Nanana	Fluttering wings.
Nā-pali	The north sea escarpment of Kauai. The cliffs.
Na-pali-kona	The leeward cliffs.
Nā-wiliwili	Port of Kauai. The wiliwili trees.
Nene	Shellfish.
Nonanona	Ant.
Nu'alolo-'aina	Hanging valley on Napali.
Nu'alolo Kai	Beach park on Napali. Seaward nu'alolo.
Nuku-pu'u	Hawaiian honeycreeper (*Hemignathus lucidus*).
Oheohe	Tall and straight.
'Ōhi'a-lehua	Indigenous Hawaii tree (*Metrosideros macropus, M. collina*).
'Olapa	Forest tree in Alaka'i swamp (*cheirodendron*). (Hula dancers were named olapalapa after the shaking 'olapa leaves that moved in the slightest breeze.)
Olokele	Land area along the south shore. Another name for the honeycreeper.
'Ope'ope	Bundle of clothes.
Pali	Cliff.
Pō'alima	Friday. Subdivisions of land worked only on Friday for benefit of the chiefs.
Pō'ele	Dark night.
Pohā	Hawaiian gooseberry (*Physalis peruviana*).
Poi	Fermented, cooked taro.
Po'ipū	Resort area on the south shore. Crashing waves.
Pōki'i	Ridge above Waimea. Younger brother or sister.
Poli-hale	State park beyond Barking Sands. Famous in the old days for its seaweed used in leis.
Puaiohi	Small Kauai thrush (*Phaeornis palmeri*).
Puhi	An old plantation town, now a new suburb of Lihue. A shark god.
Pu'u-Ka-Pele	Hill on the west rim of Waimea canyon. (It is said that the voices of menehune from here were heard on Oahu.) The volcano hill.
Pu'u Pihea	Highest peak on the rim of Kalalau.
Pu'u	Any kind of a protuberance from a pimple to a hill.
Uluhe	Hawaiian species of false staghorn (*Dicranopteris*).
Wai-'alae	Mountain stream draining Alaka'i swamp. Chicken water.
Wai-'ale'ale	Highest mountain on Kauai (5080 feet) with an annual rainfall of about 500 inches. Rippling and overfowing water.
Wai-awa	Area on Southwestern Kauai near Kekaha. Milkfish water.
Wai-koko	Beach on the north shore. Blood water.
Wai-lua	River on the east shore. Two waters, from the two forks upstream.
Wai-mea	Town in southwestern Kauai. The first landing place of Captain Cook. Reddish water form erosion of Kauai's dirt.
Wai-neki	Swampy mountain ridge above Waimea. Legendary home of the menehune. Bullrush water.
Wai-niha	Long valley on the north shore extending from Wai'ale'ale to the sea. Unfriendly water.
Wanawana	Sea urchin. Spiny.
Wiliwili	Native tree, bearing red seeds used in leis. Wind blowing from all directions.